CONFRONTING THE CHILD CARE CRISIS

CONFRONTING

THE CHILD CARE CRISIS

*It will be a great day when our schools get
all the money they need, and the Navy has to
hold a bake sale to buy a ship.*

— Child and Parent Action, San Francisco, California

Stevanne Auerbach

BEACON PRESS Boston

Beacon Press books are published under the auspices
of the Unitarian Universalist Association
Published simultaneously in Canada by
Fitzhenry & Whiteside Limited, Toronto

Printed in the United States of America

(hardcover) 9   8   7   6   5   4   3   2   1

Library of Congress Cataloging in Publication Data

Auerbach, Stevanne.
    Confronting the child care crisis.

    Bibliography: p.
    Includes index.
    1.   Day care centers — United States.   I.   Title
HV854.A94   362.7'1   78-19601
ISBN   0–8070–4152–1

For my mother, and other mothers, who used and believed in child care during World War II, and in honor of Eleanor Roosevelt, who has been an inspiration and who created awareness of and support for child care during that war, and for Margaret Mead, who contributed so much to our understanding and broader view of society, and who reminded us before she died in 1978 that "unless we can pull this fragmented world together, unless we can obtain a large vision, we are in very serious danger. For the children's sake, let us create a larger vision and pull it all together and make it work."

This book is in honor of
The International Year of the Child.

May we create a better world for the
children through our care of them.

ACKNOWLEDGMENTS

In June, 1966, I became the mother of a wonderful daughter and thus began my active involvement in child care. I remember asking myself many times during those early years, if it was so difficult for a resourceful college graduate to obtain good, consistent care for my daughter, what happens to all of the other millions of children, mothers and fathers who don't know where to turn when the need for care arises?

I had just begun living as a single mother and it was not easy on any level. Everything that I ever learned theoretically actually happened to me. During that time and for all the years of involvement that followed, I have had many people to thank for their ideas, support and, more importantly, their freely given encouragement.

Over the years I have hoped that child care services would receive the kind of attention needed to respond to and nurture childen in the way that is most beneficial to them. Perhaps through some critical rethinking of our values as a nation we will place children and the needs of families higher in the priorities of social action.

For now I want to thank:

• All of the mothers and fathers who have worked so hard not only on their jobs or at home, but in child care at their own children's centers, or in organizations, or for the lobbying efforts that have taken place everywhere.

• Those parents who shared their stories directly and honestly with me.

• All of the staff of centers and homes who do the best they can with the situation and strive to improve it.

• All of the legislators and policy makers who have cared, listened, and done what they could — often to the betterment of existing laws or regulations.

- All of the people in the field of child care whom I have met over these years and who have contributed to my understanding and determination to stay in this field.

Among these people are Mary Keyserling, Theresa Lansburgh, Bettye Caldwell, Helen Gordon, Dotia Zavitkovsky, Bill Pierce, Jean Berman, Al Shanker, Ted Taylor, Larry Feldman, Walter F. Mondale, John Brademas, Marvella and Birch Bayh, Shirley Chisholm, Bella Abzug, Evelyn Moore, Thelma Carter, Suzanne Arms, Glen Nimnicht, Jim and Pat Johnson, Irving Lazar and many others throughout the country.

- All of the fifty-five authors who contributed to *Child Care: A Comprehensive Guide* and those people involved in *Choosing Child Care: A Guide for Parents.*

- And to my dear faculty advisor, a mentor whose inspiration and efforts prodded me to write this book — Dr. Roy Fairfield.

I wish to thank MaryAnn Lash and Charlotte Raymond and others at Beacon Press who believed that the book needed to be written, and to my agents Elizabeth Pomada and Michael Larsen, who made sure it was.

This book was a labor of love given perfectly by the typists and staff of The Institute for Childhood Resources in San Francisco, Jovana Rudisill, Dena Reiner, Linda Grizner, Deon Dolphin and Mary P. Howell. Thank you for all of the hours of careful effort.

Most of all I thank my dearest daughter Amy Beth who will, I hope, one day understand why all of the sacrifices were made.

PREFACE

It often has been noted that the measure of civilization is its concern for the care of its children. Parents, the public and the government must recognize that children deserve, need and require protection and care. Adults who care about children also must be determined to do something about children's well-being, even if it means fighting for the right to raise them in a healthy environment.

Neglect of children is reflected by segregation, poverty, inaccessibility of educational opportunities, an overwhelming bombardment of television, the impact of violence and abuse, as well as lack of basic care such as maternal-paternal support, consistency and continuity of care from parents or well-chosen surrogates.

We will continue to have children, but how we have and raise them is a serious dilemma. Because children do not vote, and their parents are often unable to organize themselves, children's issues, and particularly provision of child care services, are often shunted aside. Children face many problems today, not only from their environment in general, but in their basic care and well-being as fragile filaments of this country's future. If we are concerned about our economic, social and political structure, and the future of our country and its people, then we must be concerned now about what is happening to our nation's children.

The care for children begins prior to their birth and continues right through adulthood. The nature of parents' economic situation and social, physical and psychological environment will affect the children enormously. In fact, how we treat our children from the moment of birth reflects how we, as a society, regard ourselves. If, for example, babies enter the world drugged, deprived of loving human contact, quiet and nurturing conditions, or later are abused or mistreated, is it any wonder that their subsequent development can be drastically affected? Whether we want to or not, we all share in the responsibility of child care. Bad nurturing or negative experiences result in a society that is, in fact, weakened. Look at today's schools, violence and depression. Yet, we can do something to forestall these negative trends if we are willing to join together to achieve positive results.

The availability of good quality child care has been an issue that has affected children and their families for more than twenty years. What has happened in child care services, what might happen, and what can happen, is the context of this book. *Confronting the Child Care Crisis* reports on the factors influencing the state of child care in America today. It is an attempt to cut through the public's confusion and clarify important issues. This confusion acts as a barrier to action and resolution. The book will point out some of the possible directions that can be taken at the national, state and local levels. The perspectives brought to the book have been influenced by years of work in education and child care as a professional, a mother, a stepmother, a single and married working woman, as well as a politically oriented citizen who is deeply concerned about the future of this country.

My experience has been gained from many places. I grew up in New York City, and later, while working in Washington, D.C., visited child care services throughout the country, from Boston to Oregon, California to Florida. After moving to California, I looked at the system of child care in San Francisco and California over a period of years. I have, over the years, listened to hundreds of parents, professionals, politicians, program and research specialists, all discussing, debating or just arguing the various aspects of child care. After attending countless meetings as a government employee, a doctoral student, group leader, participant, teacher, student, wife or working mother, I have noted time and again that parents are rarely given the opportunity to express their positions, political concerns, or obtain information. I, too, have felt helpless as I watched political actions taken that were less than effective, and, more often, damaging or insensitive to families, including my own.

Before it is too late, we must attempt to circumvent or

change the course of some recent negative decisions which resulted in actions that seriously hamper the health and growth of millions of children and will ultimately damage the well-being of our nation. It *is* possible to have excellent child care resources available, but it is *not* possible without everyone's attention and action.

Child care advocates have been disappointed countless times over the years because of their dependency on unstable amounts of federal funds and the resulting political ploys that have opened and closed programs. Many important services have been shut down after becoming essential to the parents who used them. As a result, many frustrated parents were left desperate and wondering what to do next.

The decisions made in Washington do affect everyone, whatever their economic level or needs. We, as a "family" encompassing all of society, are affected by these policies, programs and pressures. The fate of one group of children will, over a period of time, affect all of America's children. Let us confront the crisis in child care and create the best environment for all of our children, for the sake of what is right for now and in the future.

CONTENTS

1 WHO NEEDS CHILD CARE?

The American family today faces many complex challenges. The basic problem the family must confront is sustaining itself as a viable institution in the midst of numerous economic, social, psychological and personal pressures. There are no easy solutions but there are hopeful signs that indicate new directions.

The challenge of maintaining and providing for a family is very real for millions of people. There never seems to be enough money to clothe, feed, house, entertain or educate children. Even in the face of continued inflation, cutbacks in government spending and political dissension, the issues of child care and the continued needs of children must gain the interest and support of the public.

Our potential rests with our children. The example adults set for them now reflects how we care about them and will help them grow as responsible and loving citizens. The philosophy of child care, and world of work and the family, should be based upon a premise of mutual support, concern and responsibility.

Enormous transformations are taking place in society, and in the attitudes of women as they actively seek to re-evaluate themselves in their new roles as mothers, workers, students and responsible citizens. Millions of women have returned to work over the past decade. The necessity or interest in returning to work has forced a new definition of mother/wife/career woman on husbands and children. Men, as fathers and partners in the new working and shared home-work combination, have had many adjustments to make in redefining their own role in the family. The two partners need to find ways to share jobs at home with each other and the children. Many other millions of women, and an increasing number of men, are singly responsible for the care and upbringing of children, which poses special and different challenges for adults and children.

1

An article in the book *Toward a National Policy for Children and Family* observed:

> Any report on child development must examine the environment in which most children grow, learn, and are cared for — the family. The American family has been undergoing rapid and radical change and is today significantly different from what it was only 25 years ago. Changes in the structure and functioning of the family have significant implications for children and for all institutions concerned with their growth and development.[1]

The working woman and the changes for families are reflected in data compiled by the U.S. Department of Labor Women's Bureau:

• In 1978, 60 percent of married women with children between the ages of six and seventeen and 44 percent of those with children under six were either working or looking for work. Of those who had jobs, two-thirds were working full time.

• In 1974, there were 970,000 divorces or reported annulments involving roughly 1.2 million children. This rate is increasing sharply.

• In 1978, nearly one in every five children under eighteen was living in a single-parent family, more than double the figure in 1950.

• In 1977, more than 16 percent of American children were living in families with incomes below the government-defined poverty line.

• Of the 3.2 million children in families with incomes of less than $5,000, 60 percent live in single-parent families.

• In 1975, there were only about 1.7 million children in all licensed day care centers, Head Start programs, and approved family day care homes — compared with a total of 18.2 million children under six in the United States. About 6.5 million of these live in families in which the mother is in the labor force.

• The quality of care provided in such facilities varies enormously, and a majority of family day care homes and centers are rated as only poor or fair by observers trained to evaluate programs.

• In 1974, approximately 4.7 million children aged three to five were in some form of preschool program, 75 percent of these children were in for only part of the day. Preschool programs enrolled 79 percent of the five-year-olds, 38 percent of the four-year-olds, and 20 percent of the three-year-olds in the country.

- A substantial majority of substitute (nonparental) care in the United States is provided under informal cooperative arrangements with neighbors, relatives and friends.

- More than two million school-age children have no formal care at all between the end of school hours and the time parents return from work.

- A significant number of women do not receive adequate prenatal care, resulting in high rates of infant mortality and morbidity. Among forty-two nations keeping comparable statistics, the United States ranks sixteenth in infant mortality.

- One out of three of America's 20 million children do not receive adequate health care, including access to primary care, complete immunizations and prompt and early treatment of disease. A recent survey in Syracuse, New York, for example, showed that 55 percent of children had no demonstrable antibodies to Type 1 polio virus.

Family Pressures Are Society's Challenge

Society today places a great deal of stress on parents and children. The utmost amount of sensitivity, communication, mutual support and commitment is required to deal with the stress that affects, in varying degrees, each member of the family. How individual members of the family handle the daily pressures is the real test; the assistance the family is given is society's challenge.

Statistics can show only the surface pressures and stresses on couples, which are reflected in the increasing incidence of divorce over the past ten years. As these changes bring with them a personal, societal redefinition and restructuring of services, the results can only be constructive. The family's needs require a closer examination, and by taking these aspects apart piece by piece, we may be able to reshape services in a new and, perhaps, more effective and satisfying way.

For example, many women returning to work following divorce or death of their spouses are fully responsible for supporting themselves and their children. They are confronting many new problems. The care and raising of children are tremendous responsibilities even when two people communicate and agree with each other. But for many couples, rapid societal changes have also brought about such profound changes in their relationship that many of them choose to separate rather than handle the stress.

Vast changes are taking place in the world of work, causing additional problems for families. Many of these problems have resulted from an apparent insensitivity and lack of commitment (or follow-up) on the part of federal, state and local governments to respond to the societal responsibility of taking care of children while parents work.

The creation of, and amount of support for, ongoing child care services determine families' abilities to cope with many of these changes. Attempts to assist families often have been piecemeal efforts. Research or "demonstration" programs are scattered throughout colleges and universities, but do not result in a firm commitment to make services available. The final effect has been even more destructive to the fragile nature of the family structure and has greater potential for long-term negative effects on the children. If children who need care are to get it, an ongoing support service must be available from infancy through school age.

It is of paramount importance that our entire society reinvestigate what can be done with our current resources to find new ways to support the family through child care. If we wish to be productive, it is impossible to do otherwise. If society is, in fact, interdependent, then mutual support and understanding will build a better and more creative society. If the problems of our neighbors are considered our own, then we need to look again at new ways to assist all our children in becoming cared for, educated and eventually productive, satisfied adults. It benefits everyone to have a society in which individuals' needs are considered realistically. In other countries where a long-term support system is carried out, individuals look upon themselves and their government differently, and this difference is reflected in their productivity as members of society. If attitudes change, many other changes can take place without increasing budgets or staff levels.

Child care became critically important in this country during World War II when women were needed in the work force. During the war children were found abandoned, or sleeping in overheated automobiles, and untimely deaths occurred. These tragedies were brought to the attention of Congress by the president's wife, Eleanor Roosevelt. As a result of her concern, the Lanham Act was passed in 1942. This legislation resulted in child care services springing up all over the country, particularly around war plants. Those services helped reverse the traditional picture of a mother at home.

Dr. James Hymes, a director of the early Kaiser shipyard – sponsored child care programs, has said, "There were many additional services provided to the parents, like hot meals after work that could be taken home. There was a real concern for the child and it was expressed in the quality of the programs. . . .

"America needed womanpower to win the war. The federal government set up and supported child care centers for the children of war-working mothers."[2]

These early child care centers took their name from Congressman Fritz Garland Lanham of Texas, who introduced the legislation. As First Lady, Eleanor Roosevelt created an effective lobby on behalf of child care legislation. At the peak of the Lanham Child Care Center Program (it ended in 1946), 129,474 young children were enrolled. This indicated that in all parts of the country, serving parents from all backgrounds, America had demonstrated how a good program for young children could be conducted to the benefit of everyone concerned. The Lanham Centers, moreover, operated all day long, not just from 9:00 A.M. to 3:00 P.M. These centers were geared to working mothers.

When the war ended, parents wanted the children's programs to continue because they saw the benefits of social and educational interaction. As Bernard Greenblatt reports, "Women in New York City organized and brought strong pressure to bear on Governor Thomas E. Dewey to resume state aid for day care. They picketed his residence; he called them communists. Maternal pressure to continue the Lanham programs in Michigan after the war also led to charges of communism. Representatives of nine professional and women's groups met with and presented a series of recommendations to President Truman, for example, favoring federal aid to public schools and including provision for nursery schools and kindergartens. The meeting proved fruitless, apparently, as the mothers and preschool advocates had failed to understand that social parenthood was only patriotic during a war or national emergency."[3]

It is not simply the care of children that is or has been at issue. The controversy surrounding child care services relates to our current trends in political, economic and personal attitudes toward children. Some of these are more subtle than others. Child care affects, at one time or another, all families — welfare parents, as well as middle- and high-income families; white parents, as well as black; Spanish, Chinese and all other ethnic groups — it involves everyone who is concerned about national employment stability, family support and the well-being of children. In the end, everyone, including the employer, the political system and society as a whole, is affected by the availability or absence of child care. Without it, mothers cannot sustain themselves and children are damaged.

From this perspective, I have long seen the need to increase not only understanding of the problem but wider acceptance and willingness to do something about it. Without a commitment to carry out what yet needs to be done, it is doubtful whether the efforts made by thousands of professionals and parents throughout the country can be sustained or improved. Because children's services have been so undermined and mismanaged by political, economic and social forces over the years, many programs that might have been working favorably on behalf of families have either been closed or have been operating at minimum efficiency.

As a mother I, too, am concerned about the survival of the child care system. The present and future problems of women in this country are deeply affected by the availability of child care services and something innovative can and must be done. Shortcuts are not feasible. Concerted efforts must bring us together with the best application of national, state and local planning.

Improvement can occur if a new process is created for getting the job done from Washington, D.C. As a nation, we have in the past solved problems by taking cohesive action. There is no reason not to reach the heights in solving the dilemma of serving the best interests of our children in child care.

Selma Fraiberg explains the tremendous social costs involved when society neglects its children.

> The cost of maintaining children in poverty cannot be calculated in dollars and cents. For those who like to work out the figures, I would suggest some of the factors that need to go into the calculation. The lost and broken human connections which are the common lot of many young children in poverty are directly related to the social diseases of poverty. School failure, juvenile crime, mental instability are increased in any population in which the bonds between the children and their human partners are absent or eroded as in the circumstances of poverty. Malnutrition *in utero* and throughout the years of childhood is directly related to the high incidence of disease and early death in the families of poverty. The omnipresent neighborhood dangers and crime which every ghetto child experiences will infect a very large part of the child population and provide irresistible vocational models for the vulnerable. The climate of self-denigration and despair in the ghetto will do the rest. By the time the welfare child has reached the age of six, his net worth in cash and I.Q. will be calculated for him, and he will know it isn't much. If he survives to the age of marriage, he is likely, as the rest of us are, to reproduce the patterns of his child rearing for his own children.[4]

Money is an important resource, but not the whole problem. Political leaders' commitment and willingness to provide the actual services are vital. Social policy planners, organizations and parents themselves are other important factors. More federal funds and high program standards must be maintained to insure quality.

Certainly when women were required in the work force during times of national need, solutions to the critical problems of child care were found. The need for these valuable services did not go away, but has continued to be a problem for families. The services should be developed despite the obvious barriers.

The State of the Nation

Politicians all too frequently carry out the business of the country in the most expedient and least efficient manner possible. Legislation is often introduced and passed whether or not it will serve the people's best interests, either for the short or long term. The reality of the situation is that politicians are pressured by business, industry, and other special interest groups. As a result, many of the services that are required for the basic maintenance of individuals and families are shunted aside while other issues that appear more expedient, more politically interesting or directly compensating are addressed. Thus, the more subtle problems of families are cast aside or dealt with in unrealistic terms.

The situation today is that the family, as we know it, is undergoing enormous strains and is not getting adequate political attention. Certain trends, though, make the problems loom larger. Over the last twenty-five years, women did not return to the home after childbirth but continued working. The cost of living has increased, forcing them to supplement their husbands' incomes. In addition, many mothers became single parents, whether through deaths of their husbands, divorce or their own choice.

There is a relationship between the absence of child care services and the breakdown of the family. The lack of these services comes at a time when parents do need to work or attend school and take time to gather their own personal resources together. During these times, if politicians had the broader interests of society as their primary concern, they would make decisions on the need to improve the conditions of families. It may be that the absence of child care services, when it has been needed these past ten years since the veto and resulting lack of coordinated action, not only contributed to the breakdown of the family, but also to the higher incidence of child abuse, abandoned children and other destructive behavior toward children in this country. The attention politicians have given the abortion issue might also extend to their responsibility to unwanted, neglected children with unmet educational, health care and child care needs. Another result of ignoring these needs are the millions of teenagers having babies at the most vulnerable time of their lives.

The shifting of political support is indicative of the concerns and conflicts about child care in the past. During 1962, child care was amended as part of the Social Security Act and, in 1968, federal interagency standards were established.

In 1969, the Committee on Education and Labor of the U.S. House of Representatives was in the process of considering a comprehensive child care bill. After many, many months of hearings, expert testimony and carefully documented sources from all over the country, the legislation was passed by both the House and Senate with bipartisan support. The legislation received enthusiastic endorsement from the more than 4,000 delegates who attended the 1970 White House Conference on Children.

Optimism for the provision of expanded services was at its highest. It looked as though a national, state and local child care system that worked was in the making. Hopes were dashed when former President Nixon vetoed this legislation in December of 1971. In his statement, he noted that child care would create a "breakdown of the family."[5]

The truth is that the absence of good child care has created the demise of the support needed by the family in this decade. The results are apparent in the many problems confronting the family today. Conservative interest and pressure in 1970 came from individuals who were also against women's rights or the rights of children to have good quality care while their mothers were working. These people came together to bring pressure against this important legislation. The move came as a surprise to those who saw these services as right and just, not a matter of ideology.

Because of national politics and ongoing controversy, with its resulting confusion, child care legislation failed to overcome presidential veto in 1971 and again in 1975. In the International Year of the Child, action seemed about to be taken. In 1979 new legislation was introduced by Senator Alan Cranston of California. His strong testimony on behalf of expansion of child care services is included in the Appendix. Also included for a point of reference is the veto message of former President Nixon. It is important to understand the conservative resistance to the advances suggested by socially responsible legislation. The basic issue is still the same today: how to provide consistent, quality child care that parents can depend on. After months of hearings, the bill was withdrawn.

The need, of course, is to expand a support system that includes public and private resources: schools, business and social-services agencies of all kinds. The greater diversity, the better, but the issue of who handles the funds has become an issue of major proportion. Essentially, the country must take a broader social view than that afforded by particular groups and their self-interests, whether they are the views of the church, government, business or specific self-serving groups. Perhaps people then will begin to develop creative solutions that benefit the larger society. Those who thwart energy by finding it convenient to create negative issues around children, women or gay rights cause new problems by supporting policies that increase teen age pregnancy, cut funds for vital services to handicapped children and, inadvertently, make innocent people scapegoats.

Politicians need to be aware of falling into those old, vicious traps. Ideally, politicians are "facilitators" in the process of improving society. Their positions can stimulate and support the improvements needed by all our citizens; they should analyze positions and see the long-term support needed for these vital services, then facilitate the creation — through government or voluntary sponsorship — of the groups that are needed. For this to happen, though, federal, state and local governments must adopt a new and creative position that more adequately reflects society's concerns.

Gilbert Steiner, in his book *The Children's Cause*, succinctly states one of the drawbacks:

> Children are part of every member's constituency, and fit into no single committee's jurisdiction. The result is a distribution of responsibility for child health, nutrition, welfare, and development across standing committee lines. While a member might start from any of these perspectives and develop a general specialization in children's policy, that path is unlikely because the original toehold is both uninviting and small. Recognizing this circumstance as both reality and opportunity, Walter Mondale sought to effect new arrangements with the cross-cutting Sub-Committee on Children and Youth. But neither is it immune to the jurisdictional problem, nor can it claim important legislative successes. Locating a focal point of congressional leadership of the children's cause is no less difficult now than it was before the Sub-Committee came into existence.[6]

We also need to look at the experiences of other countries. In countries where a long-range view is taken of important issues, the resultant social policy creates programs that receive regular support. This is true for child care in a number of social democratic countries where a long-term view and support are given to the availability of child care.

In *Child Care — Who Cares*, Pamela Roby notices the difference.

> Americans entering Scandinavian or Israeli children's centers are immediately struck by their hominess. . . . American visitors to these nations are also struck by the seriousness with which their hosts explain that child-care center policies should be considered only in the context of a comprehensive social policy for the promotion of the children's well-being and development and the well-being of their parents. Many nations' provision of comprehensive children's service stands in marked contrast to the American practice of attempting to assist low-income children by providing one isolated service after another, rather than a comprehensive program of services.[7]

At the very least, our politicians might maintain some degree of impartiality in considering all sides of the issues. Self-interest groups that deny the rights of others who are less fortunate than themselves, or who are not able to handle the overwhelming odds against them, including children, old people, single parents, abused people, handicapped people and others, can cause the disintegration of the whole society.

Ideally, the concerns of children and families should not become such volatile political issues. But, with no simple solutions, they are. What has happened to the movement toward obtaining new funding for comprehensive child care programs throughout the country? Legislation could provide a much needed consolidation of programs and funds to create an expanded program for all children who need these services. Comprehensive legislation includes training teachers and providing physical facilities and health care. This type of approach is what most professionals and parent groups have been seeking. Band-aid approaches do not work over time.

Over the years, many speakers concerned about children have testified before the U.S. House of Representatives and

Senate special committees. Mary Keyserling, former director of the U.S. Department of Labor, Women's Bureau, has witnessed the need and growth of the day care movement since World War II. In her 1972 report, *Windows on Day Care*, she wrote:

> There was virtually universal agreement that developmental day care services should be greatly expanded. Almost no one with whom the issue was discussed suggested that existing services were even remotely adequate in quantity or quality. Some informed people said that were the day care available to be increased 10 or 15 fold, this would not suffice. In some critical neighborhoods it was estimated that services need to be increased as much as 100 fold. Some of those concerned with need suggested that the enrollment capacity of day care facilities be increased from 300 to 700 percent. A few geared their estimates to what seemed to them to be realistically achievable in the near future, given present resources, and expressed the view that were enrollment capacity of all licensed facilities doubled, the resulting new places could immediately be filled.[8]

According to Senate testimony of Reginald Lurie, of the Joint Commission on Mental Health and Children, in 1971:

> The child advocacy program, as we picture it, can make us aware, not only of who and where all the children are, something we don't know now, but of what they need. If the concept of child advocacy could be linked to the child care program established by this bill, we would have a more logical basis to make a determination as to what each child really needs. If we can determine what our children need, we will be in a much better position to meet those needs. And only if we meet those needs can we say we are really doing a job of protecting our most valuable resource - our children. . . .
>
> This nation, which looks to the family to nurture its young, gives no real help with child-rearing until a child is badly disturbed or disruptive to the community. The discontent, apathy, and violence today, are a warning that society has not assumed its responsibility to insure an environment which will provide optimum care for its children. The family cannot be allowed to withstand alone the enormous pressures of an increasingly technological world. Within the community, some mechanism must be created which will assume the responsibility for insuring the necessary supports for the child and family.[9]

Talk, Talk, Talk

There certainly has been no dearth of congressional testimony on the issue. After hundreds of advocates for and against child care had testified before Congress, the outlines of a possible program — its operations and provisions — became clearer.

The Office of Child Development (located within the Department of Health, Education and Welfare) was established in 1965 to bring together the programs in the offices of education, health, child development and public assistance to support the needs of all children. The benefits this approach might have provided have not yet come to fruition, though. Self-interest groups who fought to preserve their own constituent groups — Head Start, education, social work — fought each other and were never able to see the potentially powerful lobby and program they could have by finding ways to work out common strategies and programs. These efforts at consolidation were further sidetracked by the 1971 Nixon veto. The proposed child care bill went underground after that. It later emerged in 1975, only to meet with another presidential veto.

As child care is currently conceived, there are three different types of programs — family day care in homes, group day care homes and day care centers. Family day care homes are often preferred by parents of infants or toddlers who need to be in a home environment near their own. Often a family day care home meets the needs of children before and after school as well. Family day care home providers also need training, supplementary services and resources as well as back-up and support systems. They also need to be licensed or registered. Providers usually need continuous training and an opportunity to learn more about child growth and development, education, first aid, and other special needs. One system that has worked in Portland, Oregon, and in other places is a network of family day care homes where providers are kept informed of each other and can assist one another in services.

A group day care home is a slightly larger program caring for children. Again the problems are similar in that they also need back-up and support.

Day care centers are private and public, and can be located in schools, churches, recreation centers or settlement houses. They vary widely in quality. Each one depends on the staff and the resources available to that center.

Over the past twenty years, disparate programs have emerged in the movement toward creating more child care services. There are independent, private programs, as well as many child care and private nursery schools that operate independently and without public supervision. The parents who can afford these services are not dependent on federal policies, but, in the long run, they too are affected. Head Start programs operate for the most part as half-day programs. Many of the parents require full-day care for their children. It would require an act of Congress, a total administrative shift in federal agencies, and some creative new thinking to coordinate these independent services. It is this separateness that results in high costs, waste and inefficiency, plus a great deal of parental frustration. The similarities among many of the programs and the curriculum can allow for much greater flexibility and connection.

The predominant reason for connecting these services is to provide a needed flow and support for children. For example, children moving from their Head Start program into a public school kindergarten need some continuity, and this requires planning for the total child in these programs. The self-interest groups worry about the survival of their own programs, and only see their own immediate budget and power base, not the long-range needs of the child and family.

Some politicians attempted to do something about this mess in addressing child care bills in hearings. For this reason, expectations were high that progress would be made in providing better ongoing services for children. At the same time, opposing forces saw child care as a threat to their own security and survival, and both times flooded the White House with mail urging a veto. The high expectations were dashed with both presidential vetoes. More thought should have gone into the matter before the vetoes. It also is unfortunate that Presidents Nixon and Ford did not have the sense to see the larger picture at the time, or have real concern for those children who needed care. They responded solely to those against child care services, and other supporters who represented negative pressure groups.

The results have been obvious. Low-level consciousness produces low-level leadership. The vetoes resulted in many additional problems, most of which have damaged the rights of children. The cycle of poverty and continued neglect is perpetuated and creates impossible social conditions.

Now, more than one million teen-agers annually are having unwanted babies. Irreparable damage is done to these teen-agers, as well as to their offspring. The absence of child care services in the schools leaves these adolescents even more vulnerable because they cannot complete their studies. Politicians actively discuss these issues and vote against low-cost, safe abortions, yet at the same time they are not willing to provide for the later — and higher — costs of child care that are absolutely necessary to make it possible for a child to survive in this world. The vital point is not just to be born, but to be nurtured. The costs must be measured by the initial cost of $150 for an abortion compared to more than $3,000 per year to house, feed, clothe and educate a child.

Most medical people agree that girls who become pregnant before they are seventeen years old are at a great biological and psychological disadvantage, as a National Academy of Sciences report, *Toward a National Policy on Children and Family*, recently stated.

> The pregnant school-age girl is at variance with many of the expectations of the American middle class if she chooses to carry the pregnancy to completion and then keep the baby. The girls who have abortions or who surrender their infants are not penalized permanently. The "problem" centers around the school-age mother who keeps her child. In most cases, she has not yet graduated from high school; she frequently is not married when the baby is born, and she is even less likely to have been married when the infant was conceived. If the young mother is unmarried and brings her baby home to live in her parents' residence, the mother and child become economically dependent upon her parents or upon some form of welfare. American society conceivably could consider this lifestyle as an acceptable alternative . . . just as it accepts attending college and depending economically on parents as an acceptable, and even

laudatory, alternative to entering employment and becoming financially independent. But for many reasons, society has labeled the pregnant school-age girl and mother as a deviate. The deviance is a problem in proportion to its visibility and its duration. If the young mother is unmarried, white, and gives the baby up for adoption, white society tends to view this as a small problem despite the fact that it may be traumatic to the mother, because she soon can return to the expectant adolescent pattern and she has contributed to the currently inadequate pool of white babies available for adoption. Unmarried white mothers who choose to keep their infants and unmarried black mothers who are more or less forced to by the small demand for adoptive black babies, are seen as greater problems. . . .

Even if the school-age pregnancy does not result in increased welfare support, it may cause another economic problem: Premature arrival into the labor force. Under current conditions of less than full employment, there is little demand for teenage workers. The economy can be served better by completion of their high school education and perhaps continuation to college or some technical institution to gain special skills. When, as a result of pregnancy, the young mother decides to leave high school before graduation or not to seek post high school training, these decisions have an adverse effect on economic conditions because of the present structure of the labor market. The effect is similar when the putative father or young husband shortens his formal education or technical training in order to seek employment to support his chilc' or his family.[10]

It is essential to take a very close look at the interconnection and mutual dependency among legislatures, government programs, public opinion and the nation's needs. Clearly, we must be willing to overlook individual agendas in order to plan and provide improved programs for everyone. The challenge will be in doing this critically and openly without first cutting out the human services as if people do not matter.

One way to forestall action is to hold hearings. The pattern is nearly always the same. Legislators listen to the expressed needs, and then fail to follow up with any action.

The challenge is to incorporate the various recommendations into a long-range workable plan — a plan both politically feasible and supportive to the people who are affected by the availability of services. In the past, policies that were resisted or totally rejected by some groups have been carried out if the best interests of the country were involved. Child care services are as important an issue as this nation has to grapple with; it is in this sensitive area of direct response to needs that we can find the true test of our greatness.

If children are neglected; if parents are frustrated and unhappy; if employers have employees who are working inefficiently; if families are broken up from lack of support, then what have we gained as a nation in terms of our greatness or our long-range values? What does the rest of the world think when they look at America? We have been a nation torn asunder by unrest, by exploitation, by gross, inappropriate and unethical behavior on the parts of politicians who have risen to the highest offices in the land. It is time that our country speaks with a different voice and shows concern for the most vulnerable in the land. Young children have the right to protection by the state, particularly if the state declares that the right to life is of paramount importance. The state must then be concerned and responsive in creating conditions for the care and well-being of its children — not just in one specific year for one specific program, but for an entire set of policies that are guaranteed support over a period of years.

Economizing on children in a country such as ours is a disgrace. What is needed in child care are a good staff, health and nutrition, medical services and a good environment. Education must play a double role. Child care should be like a second home with a more or less set routine, including physical care which gradually tapers off as the children grow older.

A civilization is judged by the way it treats its children. The United States cannot afford a reputation that demonstrates neglect of the nation's children or of women who strive to achieve, accomplish and earn a living for themselves and their children. Whether we like it or not, working mothers are here to stay. All mothers, regardless of race or economic conditions, face the same basic problem — knowing their children are cared for while they are out of the home. Children, their mothers, and fathers need this attention as they never needed it before. Child care can be a stabilizing force in the overall drama and changing roles of family life.

2 DON'T FORGET THE PARENTS

The late Margaret Mead wrote last year that:

> The day of the extended family is over. That leaves the traditional nuclear family up a rocky, pitfall-riddled creek. Nobody has ever before asked the nuclear family to live all by itself in a box the way we do. With no relatives, no support, we've put it in an impossible situation. We need to reestablish supports for the nuclear family, to reestablish the community, and that has to be done on a nation and world scale. It's too complicated just to be done locally.[1]

Many of the problems of the family can be traced to the child care crisis. The number of mothers of children from infancy to age six in the labor force rose from 13 percent in 1948 to 41 percent in March of 1977. Seven million children of preschool age require some type of child care while their mothers are working. Children of families with single fathers also need day care. In addition, the percentage of women with children aged six to thirteen in the labor force nearly doubled during the same thirty-year period rising from 31 percent in 1948 to 58 percent in 1977–78.

Fifteen million young school-age children need some child care arrangements before and after school. Approximately eleven million children under the age of fourteen spend some time of each week in some type of day care; estimates on the national average are that there are 900,000 children cared for in licensed centers and about 775,000 in licensed or approved family day care homes; the remainder are in private baby-sitting settings. It is obvious that there is an acute shortage of licensed facilities for middle-income families. Every parent that I have ever spoken to indicated varying degrees of frustration when trying to locate child care. In 1972, the *Statement of Principles in Day Care*, published by the

Office of Child Development (now, the Agency for Children, Youth and Family) stated:

> This country stands at the crossroads in establishing new day care services and expending and improving existing services. Whatever direction such services take, the family will remain the basic unit for the care of children.
>
> Our changing society requires that other methods of day care be provided to supplement the role of the child's basic unit, while keeping the family an integral part of all day care services.
>
> To accommodate varied circumstances, day care programs must take into account certain basic factors of child development, family life and social settings which identify the conditions that enable a child to realize his potentials. The U.S. Government has a public responsibility to provide day care services for any family desiring such services. When families need to reach beyond their own kinship resources for assistance in the care and rearing of their children, they need a wide variety of arrangements for supplemental care. We advocate, as national public policy, the creation of programs to strengthen all kinds of supplemental day care arrangements that families strive to make.[2]

The principles of child care are basically sound, but what is currently available, or even what has been available over the past ten years, falls short of the ideal. The rhetoric of enabling children to meet their individual potentials seems hollow when one actually talks with a typical parent or visits children in the child care setting.

According to Mary Keyserling mothers go to work primarily for economic reasons, and without these earnings families could not get by.[3] Women struggle to make ends meet economically as well as emotionally, and it is both self-defeating and cruel for them to receive so little help from all levels of government in their attempt to locate and maintain good child care services.

The study conducted by Mary Keyserling with the National Council of Jewish Women, *Windows on Day Care,* reported the most depressing and frustrating conditions. Children were in situations unfit for healthy development. Women generally had difficulty locating child care, whether in a family day care home or in a child care center. Volunteers from all over the country had visited the centers and had reported what the conditions were. Bringing this information to the attention of the government agencies responsible for the programs caused little change. State licensing officials often visit a place once, may or may not approve it, and have very little time to work with the program in order to upgrade it. The question of quality is, of course, foremost in the minds of parents, although some parents have little or no opportunity to have much choice. In fact, there are a large number of women who are not eligible for subsidized care, but whose incomes are too low to enable them to buy good care.

The problem of finding and maintaining good care is a serious one that has not been fully addressed by political bodies at any time during the past ten years. It is unfortunate that working women who are mothers and wives have such difficult struggles balancing these roles. The lack of coordination at the federal and state levels has not made it any easier for these women.

Working Women: A Growing Trend

The need of women, of course, is not new. The Bureau of Census and Children's Bureau of the Department of Health, Education and Welfare made a survey in 1958 of child care arrangements for children under the age of twelve; it was the first time a large picture of child care was available. Most of the child care was performed by relatives in the child's own home. At that time, only one child in five was cared for outside his or her home. Many of the children were expected to care for themselves.

There are powerful forces working against women who need quality day care services. Florence Ruderman's 1968 study observed that:

> There are strong elements in our society of opposition to maternal employment, based on economic and social conservatism, ideological convictions regarding women's place, and so on. There is a general tendency to treat family questions as entirely private. There is a powerful laissez faire strain in all of American life, and, as a result, on many issues societal involvement has come much later here than in many European countries. In addition, the lack of

community concern may stem from the beginnings of day care of the charitable, or largely custodial service.[3]

Forty-seven percent of the parents in Ruderman's study felt they would use a good service and that it would be a welcome solution. Child care centers were usually preferred for a variety of reasons. Many felt it was better to have a center than individual maids or baby sitters because it was more beneficial for the children. Those choosing not to use the centers cited specific problems relating to work schedules, transportation, costs, or special characteristics of the child such as a handicap. Also, some mothers preferred having someone in their own home to help them with other services. Finding care for two or more children in the same place also was difficult. Mothers were concerned over a lack of personal and individual attention; a too strenuous or competitive environment; the danger of communicable diseases; overcrowding and understaffing; and a generalized fear that programs are not well run.

Ruderman noted that all social classes needed child care services, and all classes had problems arranging for them. The average middle-class family is likely to reflect many of the conditions that give rise to contemporary day care needs — greater geographic mobility, separation from the extended family, unwillingness of middle-class relatives to serve as regular child care agents, lack of close relationships with neighbors, and a society where assistance gradually disappears.

One of the key aspects of workable day care in any community, regardless of the sponsor, is the degree to which parents participate in the program. Parents have specific statements to make and it is important to understand their own particular situations.

I was involved in day care at the Department of Health, Education and Welfare and the Office of Economic Opportunity over the years, and I interviewed mothers in every part of the country, including Washington, New York, San Francisco, Indian reservations and rural communities. It became apparent that all mothers have basic underlying principles in common. Child care is not seen simply as a place to leave a child while a mother goes to work, but a place where trained persons know and understand the needs of children, and treat them with love, dignity and a sense of responsibility.

Are You Happy?

Some studies have shown that working mothers who are both happy with their jobs and satisfied with their children's day care arrangements, fare better in some situations than non-working mothers.

> The psychological test information gathered from fifth graders was that teachers found that the full-time steadily working mother seemed to be a positive fact in the child's social adjustment. In the context in which maternal employment is the common accepted pattern, its meaning to parents and children is quite different. The author suggests that the full-time maternal employment is a requirement of family well-being considering the economic circumstances, and as such, is respected and appreciated. After reviewing hundreds of studies, it is found that maternal employment has strains and compensations; part-time employment is successful adaptation to the conflict between being full-time housewife and the strain of full-time employment.[4]

Sally Wendkos Olds notes that the crucial question is whether mothers are happy with their lives.

> Instead of separating working and staying at home mothers, let us divide mothers in another way. In one group, we will put those women who love what they are doing, whether it is outside employment or homemaking; the others will be made up of those who are discontent at home or at work, and here, we do see differences. Study after study shows that the mothers who resent staying at home and the mothers who resent going to work, are more likely to have unhappy troubled children.[5]

Working mothers also can feel acute guilt about their children. A conflict sometimes occurs between an exciting, prestigious, well-paying job and the feeling that children need a full-time mother.

The inescapable fact is that the reasons a woman goes to work are often complex, subtle and not easily resolved. The challenge will be for the family to be sympathetic and under-standing of the woman's specific needs, and to be able to solve the entire family's problems with sensitivity and understanding.

3 FEDERAL FOUL-UP

The federal government can be a bureaucratic maze — or a catalyst for action. In the field of child care, unfortunately, the maze keeps getting more complicated.

By 1971, more than forty programs in eight agencies in some way had an influence on the child and family; none of these programs and agencies cooperated with each other. The end result of these freewheeling programs is that services for the same population are harder to provide, cost more, and have little impact on those for whom they are intended.

The federal government has funded child services since World War II, when they were administered by agencies such as the Women's Bureau of the Department of Labor, Children's Bureau of HEW and the War Administration. Because programs were originally conceived to provide for urgent employment needs, the Department of Labor eventually was given authority over many child care-related services. Employment training and child care seemed to go hand in hand. Simultaneously, the Department of Social Services Administration saw its role as providing child care services for the children of indigent welfare recipients. The Department of Health saw its role as providing for early detection and health care.

The Department of Agriculture provided food services and special aid to migrant workers. The Department of Housing and Urban Administration provided aid for the building of housing and child care centers. The Office of Child Development administered Head Start and funded research related to young children.

The National Institute of Education emerged as a catalyst for other related research. The Office of Education provided services for preschool handicapped children, research, support,

Post–Head Start Follow-Through, administered Title I programs for disadvantaged youth and other recreational and educational services.

This conglomeration of different agencies, different approaches, different programs and different appropriations was an attempt to serve low-income and poor people individually, but with no effort to necessarily work together. No policy had been developed to guide the emergence of these different programs.

What made this so frustrating was that the mechanism for a good system already was available. Title I of the Elementary and Secondary Education Act of 1965 had benefits that could be extended to children of preschool age and children of migrant workers. A day care program could have been developed as part of a Title I program.

A research study analyzing existing day care centers and staff could have been funded under Title IV of the same act. Studies were undertaken in 1970 by the Division of Research at OEO, which never utilized the information that was available at the time. They acted as if it never existed.

Meanwhile, Title II-A of the Economic Opportunity Act of 1964 allowed any public agency to provide, through a community action program, preschool day care and a nursery center for day care housed in a multiservice center. In addition, low-income people could apply for loans to establish day care centers under Title IV of that act, while Title I-B of the act permitted Neighborhood Youth Corps members to be day care aides.

Title VII of the Housing and Urban Development Act of 1965 made possible centers to house health, recreation, social and other community services. They could include day care centers, provided they were housed in the multipurpose facility.

Section 2 of the U.S. Housing Act of 1937 provided for loans to local housing authorities. These loans could be used to build community facilities that could include space for day care centers. They would have to be for the tenant's needs, but would also be available to all children in the area. The local housing authority could lease space at a nominal cost and either a public or private organization could run the center. The loans could cover up to 90 percent of the total cost of development.

Title I of the Demonstration Cities and Metropolitan Development Act of 1966 permitted day care projects to be part of the city demonstration program.

The Child and Nutrition Act of 1966 made day care centers eligible for participation in milk programs; lunches were provided through the National School Lunch Act of 1966.

Getting the Gears to Mesh

In September 1968, a thirteen agency panel was established to set minimum standards for day care facilities that received federal money. The intent was to raise and never to lower the level of day care services in any state, but federal interagency day care requirements were still not approved for five years after they were issued, and the interagency panel met infrequently. As a result, there was little connection between programs and their planning or administration. This certainly made life more difficult for people at the state and local levels.

In 1969, the Office of Economic Opportunity was given $2.5 million to create the Research and Demonstration Program in Child Care. Things appeared to be moving in the right direction. The White House conference, held the following year, clearly mandated a high-quality, comprehension program for child care. Both Democrats and Republicans in the Congress were interested. Private industry also was interested in providing child care, both as an industry-related service, and as a potential profit-making business enterprise. Additionally, many private groups, such as the YWCA, National Council of Jewish Women, Girl Scouts, churches and schools were studying ways to respond to this potentially expanded new national program. Business, industry, unions and the various professions were at least willing to listen to the issues. It was an exciting time — full of expectation for creating something new and worthwhile for children.

Many experimental programs were flourishing at the time with help from extensive research monies. Among these were the KLH Program at Cambridge, Massachusetts. Although criticized as being expensive (because of the added costs of gathering research). it was a forerunner of experimental employer-based child care services at or near the place of employment. Some hospitals, companies and factories had initiated child care programs for their employees' children. The American Telephone and Telegraph Company expressed interest, and sent representatives to the first business and industry meeting on child care in Chicago. As a result, several experimental services were set up, but they ceased when people realized that it would continue to cost money. A number of franchise operations also were beginning to emerge, raising concerns over the profiteering on children and the poor quality of the services.

In January of 1970, I began working at the Office of Economic Opportunity. One of my first responsibilities was helping to plan a joint-sponsored project called the Airlie House Conference, which was to bring together experts from around the country to develop a broad child care curriculum and provide program guides for infant care, early childhood and school-age programs.

The first plans for the conference called for inviting only a group of college and university researchers, including Burton White, Jerome Kagan and Urie Bronfenbrenner. Although these people had substantial contributions to make, it was imperative that persons involved in actual child care services, and especially minorities, be invited to participate. The planners agreed, and conference participants included practitioners such as Theresa Lanzburgh, Luis Diaz de Leon, Marjorie Grossett, Evelyn Moore, Evangeline Ward, Dotia Zavitovsky and others. These people had direct experiences to share and were able to suggest or produce materials relevant to Spanish-speaking, black and other minority children. More importantly, these people knew the realities of child care and helped develop curriculum materials and a statement of principles that enriched the entire effort. Their participation led to a cohesive unit that moved toward the day care forum of the 1970 White House Conference on Children. The participants of the forum were able to make day care the number one priority of the conference, although there were many other important issues involved.

The planning committee for the Airlie House Conference attempted to define some of the major child care issues. The logical first step for OEO was to examine existing day care services and look at ways to strengthen the successful components. We sought input from programs considered exemplary and asked for the assistance of every major federal agency that had a concern for, or potential relationship to, the child care program. The responses were disappointing and frustrating. Joint efforts might have proven immeasurably valuable, but limited vision hampered productivity and creative processes.

The Office of Education participated only to a limited extent and only in relation to the White House Conference on Children. Some staff members did help identify and describe exemplary early childhood programs, though.

The Department of Labor, in the 1970's, although very actively pursuing child care as it related to the employment of women, work incentives, employee benefits and union negotiations, was reluctant to work with other government child care programs. The Department of Housing and Urban Development did not stipulate that child care facilities should be a part of each new federally funded housing development, nor did the Indian and migrant bureaus do much to pursue possible links with child care services.

In the absence of clear direction from the White House and without definite legislative authorization, each department, bureau and agency was hesitant to become involved in child care efforts with others outside its own department.

This lack of cohesion was matched by the confusion over basic premises being examined by the Office of Management and Budget and the secretary of HEW. Should children be separated from their parents? Will welfare mothers go to work if provided with child care? Can welfare be reformed? Should infants be included in child care? How much does home child care cost and how much more would quality developmental care cost? The participants at the Airlie House Conference attempted to define the goals, curricula and procedures for the education of young children in child care, but their task called for more than just a week's conference. The group should have continued to meet and work on planning and development. This would have been a much wiser expenditure of time and money.

At the Office of Economic Opportunity, I learned the needs of many communities and felt we would be able to create effective services nationally. After visiting hundreds of child care programs, talking with state and local program directors, staff and parents, I repeatedly learned that the fault was in the delivery of the services, that monies and activities at the federal level were not developed in any logical way. This resulted in a continuous breakdown in communication, massive paperwork, and large amounts of monies spent for demonstrations that did not receive either continued support or effective, useful evaluation.

A major interest of the Nixon Administration in 1970 was relating child care to its welfare reform proposals. The idea was that child care services would help get mothers off welfare. This approach was a tremendous threat to many families who wanted a choice, since some parents wanted to be at home with their young children. Other parents did not have career counseling or training services available and didn't know if there were training courses in their own communities. A clear communication breakdown existed among the politicians, parents, and planners. Families who needed these services wanted response from state and local agencies. The discrepancies between Washington and state bureaucrats and among all the different programs were enormous.

Research and More Research

When it became obvious to the Nixon Administration that the programs were not operating effectively, the White House authorized research, not improvement, of the programs. To pull together effective programs, there had to be a total willingness on the part of every top-level administrator to provide improvements, not launch questionable research that only delayed action. Child care, the one major program that absolutely needed cooperation and interconnecting, was losing ground, and emerging as a very controversial issue. Whether it would continue to exist at all was a most challenging and almost impossible dilemma.

The director of OEO at the time, Donald Rumsfeld, took the position that little or nothing was known about day care, and that research was essential. Sufficient evidence gathered over the years from many different places had given sufficient data, though. The evidence was apparent in infant care studies at Syracuse University (and many other colleges and universities), in ongoing programs in California and school-age programs in Texas. The operational models for child care were available. The staffs of child care agencies pleaded for more demonstration and services, and less research.

Unfortunately, with the presidential veto of the child care legislation, and the general confusion that followed, the bureaucrats didn't even talk about ways to expand child care. They retreated to safe, costly and questionable research instead. This research went to an amazing number of high-priced contractors, and continued right into 1977 with a report that delegated more papers to be prepared.

The Office of Economic Opportunity, which was created to assist the poor, had been reshaped to fund high-priced contractors who produced the biggest, thickest, fanciest proposals imaginable.

It is important to understand the limitations of research. It can perpetuate problems, rather than solve them, and often is used as a stalling device to hold off action. Research is very highly regarded by many who cannot see its shortcomings, and is, of course, necessary for the perpetuation of researchers. In the case of child care, this has certainly been true.

For example, a major point was raised by the Nixon veto and this point has continued to haunt and thwart progress. Is child care harmful? Does it result in the breakdown of families? During the White House conference in 1970, Dr. Jerome Kagan of Harvard University suggested that day care was harmful to children. Others argued with him that this was not true, that day care itself was not harmful, but the manner in which it is conducted, the kind of environment, the amount of parent involvement, quality of the staff and other factors could be. These things are usually subtle and difficult to observe, let alone evaluate in any systematic way.

Dr. Kagan did, in fact, completely reverse his position about the harmful effects of child care six years later, after reporting his own study to the American Society for the Advancement of Science.

The federal government had the opportunity to provide useful service — and failed. For example, in 1970 it had five years' experience with the Head Start program. The government might have developed a comprehensive program in Head Start that would allow parents to work or go to school. It might have expanded and operated throughout the day so children would have the opportunity to attend as long as necessary. Instead, the Head Start program has had to fight for its survival. The components Head Start developed were exactly those needed for child care of any kind — strong parent involvement and broad services, including health and nutrition.

The breakdown of federal support and the lack of coordination and linkages created chaos at the local level, both financially and operationally. Competition may be good for automobiles and appliances, but not for children! Instead of pooling what was available from years of experience and creating a system that worked on all levels, the child care system toppled under the weight of federal policy and mismanagement.

Child care services all over the country fall prey to the inability of Washington to understand what goes on in the rest of the country. When I visited programs at the local level, this fact was hammered home time and again. The people I visited talked about their incredible difficulties with the bureaucratic red tape, long forms, impossible demands made upon them, high costs caused by mismanagement and lack of a sound integrated approach. In the end, these people became discouraged, and felt they had very little power over their own programs. They saw the services become dissipated due to lack of funding coordination. The breakdown in planning and administration among Washington, the states and the local communities resulted in higher costs and a waste of resources.

When costs become too high entire programs often get cut, damaging the actual services to the families. Child care services involve the welfare, health and education of children, as well as the employability of their parents. Costs for these services cannot be measured in money alone — we need to include the values of the parents' contributions to society when they are working.

Since few of the federal bureaucrats I met had any experience, or very little, working with children directly, they had no understanding of the urgent need for services at the local level, where the daily pressure is felt more keenly. Those who are parents, or who have worked with children, can understand that parents become discouraged with the lack of consideration for their basic survival needs. The incidences of child abuse and neglect, runaways, delinquency, and other damaging mental and physical effects are some of the by-products of this lack of concern for the family.

In the area of child care, the programs throughout the federal government should be consolidated and improved before anything new is added, so that monies would reach those for whom it was intended — the children. It is time for the various agencies to cease fighting among themselves so that rhetoric can be translated into reality.

A review, simplification and new strategies are needed immediately before another entire generation of children and families are lost and irreparably damaged.

4 THE STATE OF THE STATES

Considering the confusion and conflicts at the federal level, it is no wonder that when the actual plans and funds for programs finally reach the individual states, the confusion continues. One way to clear away the confusion is for state officials to make a solid commitment to child care. Only then is a diversified, high-quality program for young children possible. It can be done.

It is the state's responsibility to protect the child, but a child must be reached during the first six years with stimulation, educational services, love, nutrition and support. Many states forget that children exist, or that the services for them are inadequate and piecemeal. Actually, the states have great potential for turning around the weaknesses and overextension of the federal programs.

A state, for example, can decide to provide a comprehensive program that will benefit the entire population. Many of these improvements can be made without large sums of new money, but they do require a new perspective and a vision.

A governor or concerned legislator can work to coordinate legislation that already exists in such areas as childbirth practices, dispersion of educational information, parent education, child abuse prevention programs and services to handicapped children. States can combine Head Start, kindergarten and child development services to provide each family with maximum options. In addition, the state can monitor regulations in licensing, simplify the allocation of funds and provide technical assistance to counties and cities.

State information offices can provide resource materials from major national and local organizations and publishers. The states can inspect programs, act as child advocates and generally improve statewide communications. In California for example, creation of the Governor's Advisory Council on Child Development brought about improvements. To begin with, the council fosters public awareness of the problem and what can be done about it. It also requires government agencies to work together.

Another example is the Appalachian Regional Commission. For a period of time in the late 1960s and early 1970s, thirteen states within the Appalachian region received technical assistance, support and information on early childhood programs. The benefits were visible because the number of children being served rose.

It is important that states share information because avoiding duplication can save a great deal of wasteful expenditures. Programs in Maryland, Massachusetts, Illinois, South Dakota, Texas, California and Oregon demonstrate how child care activists, concerned citizens and responsive politicians can push through legislation that produces positive results.

States should look seriously at their credentialing procedures for staffworkers in child care, and provide more flexible and part-time opportunities for employment. It is also important for states to look at licensing specifications. But the foremost necessity is to look at what services are being provided to children. Are pregnant teen-agers being allowed to study and complete their education? The choice here is related to the issue of abortion. If the state is indeed responsible, it must bear and share the responsibility to provide for those people who have young children and need child care but cannot afford to pay for it from their meager wages.

Let us not fool ourselves that we are loving children by allowing unwanted children to come into the world. If we believe that a child has the right to be loved, nurtured and supported and to grow up into a fully effective and productive citizen, then we must look at what we are providing this child from the moment of birth. There may not always be two loving, smiling parents ready to welcome the child into the world. Perhaps there is only one frightened teen-ager whose parents cannot provide for her — let alone care for an additional infant. Or there might be a single mother who has been abandoned by her husband or boyfriend, or the mother who has had little or no preparation for the transition into motherhood.

The state has been designated to oversee education. Its performance is but a measure of the shortcomings of our country's policies and programs for children. A state that provides the best for its citizens is measured by a government that listens to and responds to its citizens, and by politicians who are creative and supportive. Political corruption is no more than a reflection of people's corruption and lack of moral leadership. If the corruption erodes the basic social and educational system, then we set an example for our children that will demand no more than corruption from them.

Possibilities for Coordination

The states can coordinate efforts in many areas. They can bring together legislative committees for child growth, development, education, health and social welfare. The committees can review and analyze existing state legislation, or see how children are being provided for and determine if adequate resources are being provided. And states must determine who is or who is not paying a fair share of the tax burden.

Many excellent, experienced specialists are available to review and analyze how federal social policies and proposals will affect the states' programs. A number of states jointly can bring these specialists together to conduct a critical review of federal legislative proposals and determine how they will affect the states' services. Research needs to be looked at carefully to see how it affects the states and their programmatic considerations. The Board of Cooperative Educational Services operating in New York state has done this effectively. County by county, services come together where they are needed. The Appalachian Regional Commission used this approach also. Later 4C (Childcare Community Coordinating Council) was intended to create and improve comprehensive services.

Of course, each state's problems are different. What works in Georgia may not work in California; in the same way, California's solutions are going to differ from Georgia's. But if we know that

Texas, California and New York have somewhat similar problems, it is beneficial for the state officials in those areas to exchange experiences and technical information.

It will be necessary for the states to better utilize federal, business and industry resources. The telephone company, for example, should make its services available to organizations that serve children and help them provide more services. If it does not want to spend the millions of dollars it would take to provide child care for its operators, perhaps it can provide a public service by offering telephone service at a greatly reduced rate. It takes a governor and legislators willing to put themselves on the line for children to initiate such programs.

An active children's lobby can be effective in supplying facts to government officials and reviewing priorities and programs. For example, superintendent of education Wilson Riles established the California Commission on Child Care and Development Services. Some very effective people are on the commisison, people experienced in day care since World War II, as well as those who are currently providing community services in day care homes and centers. They represent all of the different ethnic groups. Its first act was a statement of purpose:

> We believe the broadest possible community commitment and involvement is necessary to ensure quality childcare and development services. To this end, the Commission will build on the strengths of existing programs. It will also make recommendations which allow for parental choice, reinforcement of cultural values and a variety of services which support, enrich, and extend existing and proposed new services. [1]

The commission reviewed and assessed the census and other estimates to learn the number of children currently in child care services, where the services were and the number of children still in need. It looked at children under the age of three, from three to five years and five to fourteen years. Its report recommends that all families should have access to child care and development services that meet their needs. The commission developed a five-year plan to phase in new, and expand existing, child care services. The plan calls for maintaining all existing public services, letting parents choose care that is affordable, whether it is in a center, a family day care home or in their own home.

The commission decided on the following level of priorities: care of infants and toddlers; care of children of school age for before and after school care, and during holidays and vacations; resource and referral agencies, which need attention because of the need to increase communications between public and private sectors; that isolated geographic areas that have few programs should be given a priority for expansion; that child care services for handicapped children be expanded; and that parental choice should be more informed.

Other recommendations are that programs be expanded to migrant children, and that programs be maintained for state pre-school, general child development, campus child development, alternative child care, school-age parenting, infant development, exceptional children's needs and part-day needs. Sick children should be provided with programs along with emergency and respite care. All programs should enhance and reflect the cultural and linguistic backgrounds of the children enrolled. Additional services would provide appropriate contact persons and supervision for fourteen- to eighteen-year-olds when their parents are unavailable.

Funding, the commission feels, should be integrated among state, federal and local agencies. Specific recommendations are: easy access to funding, expansion of capital outlay, reimbursements for special needs, reducing parent fees, funding campus child development programs, incentives to employers to establish child care, funding salaries and benefits, preventing cash flow problems and no further reduction of federal funds.

To provide a statewide delivery system, the commisison recommends: an office of child development to administer all child care and development programs; an external review committee to assess coordination and future administrative structure; and resource and referral agencies to help parents choose appropriate care, offer support service, technical assistance and assist in coordination of community resources.

The Problems Are Everywhere

Obviously, this approach in state programs is a long time coming when reports have indicated for years that these are the basic principles needed to provide good, humane services. A report by the National Council of Organizations for Children and Youth assessed some of the country's problems in 1976. It indicated the following six states with the largest problems contained three fourths of America's children: California, Texas, Illinois, New York, Pennsylvania and Ohio.[2]

Former Governor Russell Peterson of Delaware said in 1969,

> No other area needs greater emphasis than early childhood education, although most public officials and educators acknowledge the importance of the pre-primary years, there is no consensus as to what kind of or how much training should be offered, etc. Although many states have established compulsory kindergarten programs and are offering more and more preschool opportunities, there is a shocking lack of analysis of actual operating capital costs, short- and long-range remedial benefits, teaching needs and possible program alternatives for youngsters during this formative primary year. It is encouraging, however, that states and the federal government are beginning now to slowly develop the programs offered under various public and even private auspices and to explore the possibility of expanding existing programs.[3]

Robert McNear, forner governor of South Carolina, discovered many problems when he tried to create more kindergarten programs. In Arkansas, the Governor's Council on Early Childhood Development brought together twenty-four citizens representing different geographic regions and designed proposals for executive and legislative action, developed programs to educate the public and helped coordinate services and programs. It successfully removed a constitutional restriction on the ages of children eligible for public education and established and enforced minimum standards. A state community coordinated child care program (4C) was developed and recognized as the official coordinating state agency.

Massachusetts has a long-standing commitment to day care; it has put a great deal of energy into state and local coordination and the improvement of the delivery system. Under the leadership of former Governor Francis Sargent, procedures and policies were improved and new emphasis was given to state services for children.

The experiences in these states can serve as a guide to others. An article by child care consultant Polly Greenburg suggests several low-cost state strategies that would be useful. These include guidebooks for parents, curriculum guides and materials, promoting the use of information at home through demonstrations, training unemployed parents, expanding the use of libraries and reading readiness programs, developing and supporting accessible parent cooperatives, building a volunteer and student staff and providing support for the home centers as well as expanding and improving funds that are allocated for child care.

"Apparently no state is ready to provide a uniform system of quality day care and early education complete with all related services to every eligible child, but it doesn't have to be all or nothing," Greenburg points out.[4]

Gwen Morgan, active in promoting child care in Massachusetts, suggests that when the IVC concept of day care and child development began, funds for staff activities were available under Title IVA of the Social Security Act, but HEW was slow in approving the guidelines for and use of the funds.[5] Until pilot programs in thirteen states received funds, it took a long time to develop a strong organization with incentives to organize and bring about a better way to use all the available money. Unless coordination happens at the federal level, it is almost pointless for the local communities to organize.

The Office of Child Development, for instance, administered specific Head Start funds. As a result, the staff was not working with other service agencies that needed coordination. Communication between the states and the federal government is essential in planning and maintaining consistency in the delivery system.

The challenge for the states is to look again at what can be done realistically, given a finite amount of time and money. The states can adapt many of the basic principles of programs and services and learn from each other. It would probably be useful for each state to document and then publish what services it provides for children. Workshops, training and other activities would also be useful.

It is time to move closer to the local scene so that growing problems do not prevent communities from dealing with the situation. The community is where the buck stops; unless services are improved at the federal and state levels, it is doubtful whether the local community can solve its problems alone.

Gilbert Steiner of the Brookings Institution has given his opinion on why child care programs face the problems they do.

> Not for the first time, public programs affecting children are being considered within a policy framework other than child welfare. . . . Those involved hear very little about the lifestyle of welfare's 7½ million children, but a great deal about the lifestyle of their mothers and about relieving the state of the high cost of public relief. It is readily accepted for aid and services to children and youth whose health and welfare cannot be assured without government intervention. But there is not universal agreement on where such intervention should be offered, where mandated, and where avoided in a democratic society that emphasizes the privacy of family life and worries about the dangers of state control over child development. A good many people simply ignore the issue because intervention policy in child welfare in the United States affects only a limited number of families. Public intervention is thus far no issue at all for the overwhelming majority of American children. They are provided at home by their natural parents, spend their pre-school years and after school hours in and around their own home, are fed adequate nutritious meals at home, etc.[6]

A city can plan a child care program not too much different from its Head Start program, financing child care for the welfare poor with Title IVA money. Using comparable financing, a state can establish a two-tract system offering Head Start children comprehensive care and Title IVA children custodial care. Still, there continue to be confusion and lack of coordination among federal programs. It is no wonder that the federal policies create confusion for the states and make it more difficult to provide actual services.

The Education Commission of the States exists to further working relationships among state governors, legislators, and educators for the improvement of education. It has found that federal programs often complicate state efforts and that the same duplication and rivalries seen on the federal level are often reflected in a particular state, or have been created by the differences in program operation. Many of the programs initiated in

Washington require state approval and matching funds. The states are left with the major problem of providing their own early childhood education programs for the handicapped, day care, and other services for children.

States Are Involved, Like It or Not

To a large extent, states already are involved in early childhood programs. Seven states mandate kindergarten programs, and forty-two have legislation permitting them. Thirty-nine states make some form of state aid available for kindergartens and at least three provide funding for preschool programs. Much of this increase in state activity has come about through federal government support. Children need support early. Failure in these critical early years can lead to a reduction in children's ability when they are in elementary school and can later cause a high incidence of dropouts. Children need not be retained in special classrooms if they are reached early. In the long run, it is to the advantage of all states to provide for early education programs.

Every state has had experience with Head Start programs, Title I, Follow Through, special education and other services initiated by Washington. It is unfortunate that there is not more effective sharing in these areas, within states as well as between states. Although every state recognizes the need for day care, many of them have not been able to provide for a comprehensive ongoing program. Part of the reason is the controversy about whether schools should provide child care. James Gallagher, director of the Frank Porter Graham Child Development Institute in Chapel Hill, North Carolina, said,

> Take the state of North Carolina, less than ½ of 1% of the money alloted for day care or for education goes toward research, toward trying to find out how to do the job better. People complain that the school systems are not doing their job, that day care is not doing its job, that we are spending less than one penny out of every dollar trying to find new and better ways of how to do it. If you are seriously concerned about childhood development and education then why not put the same amount of money into this field as we now

put into medicine, agriculture, and business? If we put as little money into research and development in General Motors as we have put into education or day care or child development research, they would be out of business in ten years. Businesses know what works, they know that if you make a major investment in finding systematic ways to do the job better, you get payoff from it. This is something we have not learned in the field of human resources and that we have not committed ourselves to.[7]

Dale Bumpers, when governor of Arkansas, said,

The conglomeration of guidelines and eligibility requirements that comes down to state and local levels often seems designed to keep children from getting services rather than making such services available. The cutbacks, the veto of the comprehensive childcare legislation and the off-again on-again directives of the last two years (1971) have contributed to a national policy with regard to children that can only be interpreted as negative.[8]

Many states have established an office of child development as an independent state agency. This office can include the directors of the departments of health, mental health, welfare, social security, education, vocational education, and higher education. An office of child development can coordinate all the disparate programs at the state level.

At the state and community levels, 4C committees should be composed of parents, providers of services, child development experts, and representatives of the different agencies. Another alternative is to establish a child care coordinating council in the governor's office and have the governor appoint the council. It should include parents as well as representatives of public agencies and private groups. Such an action in West Virginia created the Interagency Council on Childhood Services. An alternative is the example in Massachusetts. There the governor's office often gives the state's early education project the authority to implement its programs.

Statewide coordination enables a state to encourage industry participation in day care through a combination of state matching funds and incentives.

An example of a state providing training in one of its cities comes from Seattle, where a career ladder for day care personnel is offered. Level-one trainees attend local community colleges. On level two are intern teachers who are expected to continue their educational studies. Assistant teachers who have had three years of experience or forty-two college credits are on level three, and the position of head teacher (level four) requires a minimum of two years' experience and forty-five credits toward an associate of arts degree. The career ladder for day care home mothers is similar, with three levels. One mother with little or no background can move through all three levels in three to five years and earn a certificate.

It is necessary to look at alternatives and creative ways to resolve the problems rampant in the field of child care. It is apparent that the states act or react in accordance with the guidelines set by the federal government. If those guidelines are unclear, confusing or in conflict, the states do not move in positive directions. Clearly the ideal system would serve the children and get away from the red tape, the bureaucratic struggles and the limits placed on the services at all levels. Let us hope that before another generation of children suffers the same consequences as children have these last ten years, this dismal situation can be reversed. But it can only happen if citizens are informed and are willing to effect change at the local and state levels. State legislators need to be informed of the people's desire for improved, coordinated, flexible and well-funded child care services. Child care in this country has not yet come into its own at the state level. This is one of the challenges that lies ahead.

5 MAKING IT WORK ON THE LOCAL LEVEL

The buck stops at the local level. Each community must accept responsibility for making child care work for its citizens. The problems, shortages and aspirations of those who are involved in child care services become sharply focused when any community is observed and studied firsthand.

At the local level the end of all of the parts of the larger connections come together: funding and regulations coming from Washington, the state directions and channeling of funds toward specific program needs, the involvement of politicians and then all of the community and individual pressures. The services, as a result, will vary widely from city to city, based on the program director's ability to organize programs, best utilize funds, and gain the interest and participation of all of the professional and parent groups involved. To create an effective program, it is necessary to involve all of these participants. An office of child care or children's services established in the mayor's office can help coordinate and bring about pooling of resources and energy. If one takes a city-wide or countywide view of the problem and if specialists and resources that are available within a community are used effectively, one can create a commission, committee or office for services that has enough clout to get the job done well, be connected with parents' needs and respond to their specific aspirations. Such a program can operate effectively, given resources, space and staff.

Many issues continue to plague the local child care scene. When potential conflicts are not recognized or resolved, they inevitably grow. For example, public school systems throughout the country continue to be criticized. The public schools have many faults and many problems that are inherent in the system, but we are all responsible for those problems. The more we pull away and form alternatives to public school education, the more the public schools will continue to be weakened. The schools require the community's support and willingness to maintain the pressure for improvements. Changes can come about when enough public pressure is applied.

The possibilities the public schools hold are tremendous. They can coordinate all of the educational, health and social services within the local school. For example, parents can obtain information on resources to help their families with health and education. A parent library with educational materials might be made available. Workers and volunteers in child care programs can be trained in the community they will serve. Courses in child growth and development and parenting education can be offered in every high school. High school students themselves can visit and work in the elementary schools' child care centers. Senior citizens and volunteers can work in the schools and provide back-up and support services.

Many approaches can be tried out at the local level because the need is great. Invariably, better infant care, increased pre-school programs and expanded before- and after-school programs are needed. A system of child care that does not include the public schools does not make sense. The schools belong to the people and must be reclaimed by them.

Integrating Care

Bettye Caldwell, who has been a leader in infant education and child care, describes a project in the Little Rock, Arkansas, school district called the Kramer project.[1] This program gave children the opportunity to continue education from preschool through school age. The school day was extended and daycare was provided within the same facility. Funds came from Title IVA and the University of Arkansas and local school district cooperated with each other. By developing trust between the university and school staffs and involving the families, the organizers discovered that it was possible to develop a positive program in a public school setting. The key to success, according to Caldwell, is integrating the program with regular school activity and not permitting it to be viewed as something alien.

If the school system is to be reclaimed, education needs other support services to be effective. It makes a great deal of sense to find ways to connect school programs with other general support services such as CETA (Combined Employment Training Act) and organize them in a way that fits each community. With a cooperative approach, children feel the concern and interest as well. Child care switchboards can operate near schools or out of available school space and can keep in touch with members of the network in other parts of the city. In addition to improved communications many benefits appear, such as cutting down on wasteful travel.

The challenge is to be more creative and yet apply what we know in solving human problems of the child care crisis. The challenge is to examine more closely the findings of research, investigate the elements of good programs, gather descriptions of programs that work and see what aspects make them work.

Adults vary in their skills, interests, philosophies and approaches to life. Children vary also. Some children require more time and do best in smaller programs. Some programs put more energy into general development and physical activity, others stress reading readiness. Because children's needs vary, it cannot be assumed that any one program is good for all children. Any single approach will not be a panacea. What is important is how best to support the individual child's needs at a particular moment.

These connections do take place, and can be positive. James A. Levine reports on programs that have worked in Oakland, California, in Brookline, Massachusetts, in Atlanta, Georgia, in Austin, Texas, and in South Carolina.[2] What is important is that good services can occur wherever there is a commitment to bring about changes.

Levine sheds some light on the debate about parent control. Parents are limited in the amount of time and energy they can spend after work at meetings. When home and family needs have to be attended to, involvement in children's school is extra. Given that, they still want to know that the child's best interests are being taken care of and that they can communicate with the staff.

They want to be understood and have the opportunity to express their feelings and intentions. Some parents can and want to become more involved. Often bureaucracies restrict parent control or involvement, but it is not true that parents cannot be involved. Levine concludes:

> The arrangements worked out will no doubt vary from community to community based on the capability, power and influence of schools, other agencies and parents — that is in the short term the matter of prime sponsorship will be played out at the local level in terms of community politics not national politics . . . . A national system that respects such diversity among children, parents and communities is likely to be the most responsive system. All of this speaks for pluralism, choice, alternatives, and for a diversity of child care administrative and programming patterns as well. Not easy for policy makers but probably better for children.[3]

The most important issue at the local level is ensuring that parents find what they need when they seek child care, and that they are able to maintain employment or education. One way to facilitate this is to develop community services called "switchboards." These are link-ups between providers and the parents. They provide newsletters, information, and a support system. They refer parents to available spaces and can also provide training and linkages between different child care workers.

Another service that works is an office of children's services in the mayor's office. This office can coordinate and support funding, provide information and deploy equipment and supplies. People wishing to make contributions can be referred to places that need materials or equipment. If a parent is involved in a parent co-op and needs toys or ideas for low-cost playground equipment, a coordinator from the mayor's office can assist them in getting the information.

A parent hot-line is another important service. Families who are having difficulties can call someone trained to provide assistance. It is important that parents are not left with no one to turn to when in crisis. When this situation arises, the children suffer. The high incidence of child abuse can be greatly reduced if we provide hot-lines and other back-up support services to families. These should be provided without judgment or penalty.

When parents know that there is someone they can call and talk with, it makes all the difference to their own well-being and that of their children.

It is important that the city or county issue licensing requirements and provide other information to new family day care providers, so people who are interested in participating can in fact participate. Sometimes their need is for financing, sometimes training. It is important to be able to direct people to the information they need.

Determining Quality

It is sometimes difficult to determine the quality of a center or home at first glance, but at least the following ten questions should be asked. They can go a long way in determining whether parents and children will be satisfied with the services offered.

1. Can the place be reached easily?
2. Is the place safe, comfortable and attractive?
3. Does the place have plenty of good and varied toys and equipment for fun and learning?
4. Do the children and staff interact happily and communicate easily?
5. Does the place offer nutritious, tasty meals and snacks?
6. Is each child respected as an individual?
7. Does each child have the opportunity and space for a wide range of activities, either for playing with other children or for playing quietly by himself or herself?
8. Are my needs for the caregiver to be dependable and to value me as a parent considered?
9. Can I afford the fees at this place?
10. Is the place suitable for my child and my situation?

Ideally, each community should have a special section in the library on child care materials and early childhood. Alternately, an information referral center or the office of children's services should have a collection of the most useful materials in the day care field. This information is enormously valuable because people should not waste time duplicating activities and services that have already been created elsewhere.

Current needs and up-to-date assessments can be maintained at the local level. Training and other support services can be developed and improved. Professionals who are concerned with early childhood can participate. Organizations like the Association for Childhood Education International, or National Association for the Education of Young Children have active members and groups throughout the country. Organizations for parents involved in day care are more difficult to create, mainly because organizing for this requires an ongoing support system for the organization itself. The Day Care and Child Development Council of America has been a barometer of the situation of day care throughout the country, and it has had its own problems both in organizing and maintaining services. With increases in child care services, this organization could be active locally, but with funding cutbacks the respective organizations and activities around the country also suffer.

Another specific and useful service at the local level can be the development of a roster of supporting consultants. This would include specialists who can provide assistance to day care centers and homes in the areas of health care education, licensing, design of facilities, program development, parent involvement and other specialized fields.

The quality of services and standards can be maintained through the local office of the Department of Health, Education and Welfare, but it is also important to have a team of concerned citizens who are trained and able to go out and visit programs regularly. It is best not to leave the maintenance of programs exclusively to the professionals. Parents could turn to a community ombudsperson if problems arise.

It is recommended that when implementing regulations, information be provided for the step-by-step procedures for acquiring a license. The licensing function can be placed in an agency that is directly concerned with children's services. Specialists who become licensing monitors are trained in regulations and are given technical assistance. A coordinating board should be established to eliminate contradictory regulations. Performance standards should be flexible, and levels of acceptable compliance should be built into regulations. It is absolutely necessary that recommendations, goals and planning be provided. Providing consultants

and technical assistance is very important to assure the quality of
the services.

Infant care is essential to many parents who must return to
work shortly after the baby is born. Infant care is not yet consistently available. Although many models exist and good programs
have been operating over the years, it requires a great deal of
thought and commitment to develop programs for babies. The
physical environment must be modified. It is important that more
programs be developed. Throughout the day, adults can provide
good warm nurturing to babies, stimulating them, supporting
them, and providing for their needs. The environment should be
warm, pleasant, interesting and varied. The adults must talk to
the children frequently. The children's needs must be responded to.

An additional great gap in child care is before- and after-
school care. Many children require supervision and attention
during these times. Also, school vacations lasting from one to two
weeks or more pose problems for parents who are not always able
to take off from work. Family day care homes can provide some of
this care. In addition, the public schools can coordinate with the
Boy Scouts, Girl Scouts and recreation services. Many creative
programs can happen, but only when the community is aware of
the need and decides to do something about it. Almost any program can be improved, whether with additional materials, staff or
new ideas. It is important that the administrators of current
programs are willing to take a good look at what they are doing and
how the programs can be improved. Involving teenagers, senior
citizens and retired persons in the services for young children
benefits all groups.

The community also must respond with sensitivity to developmentally disabled children who need supervision, care and involvement in child care. The more often they are with normal
children, the better for all children. If special problems arise,
though, it is necessary for the child to be with a person who has had
sufficient training. Developmentally disabled children do not want
to be pitied or overindulged; they need to have an opportunity to
fully participate.

Now more than ever we need to take a good, hard look at
what we are doing for children at every level in our country. Most

of all, we need to focus our attention where children are. If we begin there and develop the services that children need, we would be responding to them in the most productive way. In the long run, every community stands to gain from the sensitive and sustained support of its children.

6 ONE COMMUNITY'S TRIALS AND TRAVAILS

San Francisco is a microcosm of the country in its cultural and ethnic diversity, population, urban problems and unmet needs. In 1971, I began my doctoral studies and thus had an opportunity to view child care in San Francisco from a new perspective. It is one of the ten cities in the country that houses the regional office of HEW and other federal agencies. It is a city that maintained ongoing state-supported early childhood and child care programs sponsored by the public schools. Each community had a Head Start program reflecting the various ethnic groups. The city needed and had a reasonable opportunity to develop one of the most comprehensive, ethnically balanced, quality programs anywhere. The support for child care already existed in the city, as did the possibility of cooperation among the school system, other state-funded programs and federally funded programs such as Head Start. The legislature conducted several studies analyzing the child care situation, and other studies reported the need to expand children's center programs. All of the interest pointed in the direction of increased support on the part of the community.

A children's council was created and it has expanded over the years. The Child Care Switchboard expanded from a neighborhood project that was first established to help single parents, to an organization providing a unique service throughout the city linking parents and providers.

A proposition calling for the establishment of high-quality, low-cost day care for all San Franciscans passed in 1974, but a lack of action and support by federal and state agencies created a vacuum. By 1976, the voters reversed their previous decision and voted no on the same proposition. The momentum had begun to build up. All that was needed was sufficient reinforcement. Instead, the programs teetered on the brink of disintegration. For example, a vital center for children whose parents had abused them was threatened and then was closed due to lack of funds. Programs that served children were being cut. Children were left at the bottom of the priorities list, and eventually people became frustrated, tired and burned out.

In reviewing the problems and recalling the experiences of this one community, I realize they also reflect the experiences of many other communities throughout the country. I have seen the child care services in San Francisco, which rank with the best, also have some of the worst problems.

A study of San Francisco I made in 1971 and 1972 helps illustrate the nature of child care at the local level. By understanding the local community level, it is possible to understand why diversity is necessary, what kinds of cooperation are necessary, and how to compare the child care system to other communities.

A Long History

Child care in San Francisco began in 1872 when Mrs. Alice Tobin bought a large house on Pine Street to care for children under the auspices of the Sisters of the Holy Family. In 1879, the Golden Gate Kindergarten Association began operating schools in the city. In 1909, programs were opened specifically to care for children of women working in the canneries. However, not until World War II were day care centers given serious consideration. Centers and homes were established, many provided by the local school district. Most of the day care centers that are still in existence are still sponsored by the San Francisco unified school district as part of a larger Children's Centers Program throughout the state. In addition, there are Head Start programs, nonprofit centers, private programs and family day care homes.

To learn firsthand what was happening in San Francisco, it was necessary to visit and talk with a representative sample of centers, homes and parents. To do this, I developed a special survey and interview format for parents and a follow-up interview for providers. Questions developed specifically for the directors helped discover more about the programs themselves and provided a basis for comparison.

The confusion inherent in the programs in San Francisco, as in any other large city, is related to the overlapping, and often confusing, regulations and services provided by different federal and legislative programs.

In 1965, with the passage of the Economic Opportunity Act, Head Start was created, and with it, an entirely new bureaucracy involved with communities. Many of these Head Start programs began solely as summer programs and expanded into part-day or full-day programs. It made economic sense for the poor to have an opportunity to obtain training and education simultaneously. The Model Cities Act of 1968 added a day care component. The Social Security Act enabled states to apply for funds under Title IVA. So three different pieces of legislation affected four different agencies, all with their own regulations, and all operating independently of one another. Under Title IVA, each dollar of seed money appropriated for child care by the city, a foundation or the United Bay Area Crusade would be matched by three dollars of federal funds. In addition, the state-supported Department of Education programs continued operating independently.

Of course, as the cost of college and other training increased, so did the income requested by certified teachers. The career ladder widened so that within the state staffs had varying credentials for a growing number of jobs classifications. Qualifications for Head Start teachers, child development associates, or early childhood teachers also differed.

The Department of Education operated its program independently of the community, and the community felt that the school system was hostile or indifferent to its needs. The bridging over of the cooperative spirit did not really occur except in a few programs.

Seven types of day care were available at the time. The San Francisco Unified School District operated thirty-one centers. Initially sponsored under the Lanham Act during World War II, the programs have been funded through the state Department of Education, primarily within the Division of Compensatory Education since 1965.

The 1,900 available spaces were allocated on the basis of eligibility requirements stipulating low income, with first priority to single heads of households. Parents paid approximately one fourth of the cost of the operation. The unique and special feature of the program was that school-age children could be supervised at the centers before and after regular school hours. The service was important, but fell far short of meeting the needs of the thousands of children who required supervision. Parents participated in the programs through meetings and the Parent Advisory Committee.

The buildings in most cases were old and in need of renovation, repainting and decoration. The play yards lacked adequate equipment. The programs were staffed by credentialed older women who managed a carefully supervised, structured environment; few men worked in the entire program. Breakfast was served to those who needed it. Health care was given through the visits of public health nurses, although sick children were sent home. Parents generally were satisfied with the supervision and care their children were receiving but some, non-English speaking families felt alienated or intimidated by the lack of bilingual staff.

An important supplement has been the State Preschool Program. About 500 children have been served each year in a half-day kindergarten preparation program similar to Head Start. The consultants from the school system were based in Sacramento, rather than in the community being served, which hindered continuity and seemed like an enormous waste of travel.

The Department of Social Services operated twenty-one centers from the county and state offices, with funds from the Social and Rehabilitation Service and HEW. These centers were designed to serve low-income families to enable them to seek and maintain employment, and had to meet HEW regulations and guildelines.

Head Start operated six centers, supposedly offering education, medical care and social services. The centers served thirty to fifty children, and most were overcrowded. The degree of supervision, parent involvement, training of staff, responsiveness to parents, communication and services to children varied widely among the centers.

Model Cities and a neighborhood coalition operated the

Mission Child Care Consortium to serve families who lived in the Mission District. The programs made available a range of services, including a drop-in infant center. Meals, medical services and community liaison workers were provided. Parent participation was heavily emphasized, and the staff was fully bilingual. The parents expressed their preferences on staff and personnel. The consortium offered before- and after-school programs.

Two centers have been operated by the Sisters of the Holy Family since the first child care center began in San Francisco more than 100 years ago, and were located in the Mission and Chinatown. The sisters and lay teachers supervised the largest single agency in the city, one center serving 200 children and the other serving 300. Discipline was strict and the parents participated very little. No one in either center spoke the prevailing language in the neighborhood and few extra services were offered. The nurse refused to admit any child showing any sign of illness at morning inspection. Although the programs were among the oldest in the city, they were rigid in outlook, and the staff was uncooperative.

Twelve proprietary centers and several schools offered full-day services. One that did — and that cooperated with the study — was Presidio Hill, started in 1917. As a private school that opened its enrollment to a cross section of the population, from poor to wealthy, it contrasted with centers solely for low-income families. Most parents in this school pay the full tuition, plus a fixed amount for after-school care. The hours did not always match some of the parents' work schedules, nor was the program always in accord with the parents' outlook, values and wishes, but it functioned in the way the public school extended day program attempted to, and certain aspects of the program provided a model for other private schools in the area.

The Department of Social Services licensed 300 homes in two regular categories and six in special categories (six to ten children). Some of the homes that were studied were truly warm, stimulating and homelike, while others functioned merely as dreary repositories for neglected children. This does not detract from the contention that a network of well-regulated family day care homes offers, perhaps, the greatest potential for meeting the many and varied child care needs of parents.

One woman ran a particularly good home. Her experience demonstrates the pluses and minuses of family care. What a center offers that she cannot are: (1) space — the children have no room to run around and no physical action toys; (2) more services, such as health programs and follow up; (3) outside resources and stimulation, such as trips out into the community, airport, post office, zoo, etc.

What she provides that a center might not are: (1) a sense of security and safety for the child; (2) a calmer atmosphere, because it is a home with only three to five children; (3) greater individual attention for each child; (4) the provider is directly responsible to parents; there are no conflicts among staff, director, parents and board of directors, matters that frequently plague centers.

An Exhaustive Study

During the course of the study, I visited many of the 150 child care facilities and 300 licensed family day care homes, as well as several unlicensed facilities and homes. From this number, I narrowed the list down to fifteen centers and five homes based on their sources of funding, their locations in the city, and the socio-economic characteristics of their customers. I focused on parental needs, desires and expectations. I examined, but did not emphasize, program content, philosophies and methods of the child care providers.

Almost unanimously, mothers wanted their children to spend at least part of the day outdoors. The types of outdoor play areas varied strikingly. Some were small, covered with asphalt, surrounded by chain-link fences and consisting of a few commercially manufactured and often rusty swings and slides. Others sparkled with imagination as a result of the creative use of cast-off items, such as barrels, scrap lumber, large appliance cartons, old tires and simply holes in the ground and piles of dirt. Since outdoor space is at a premium, some centers have none of their own. While some programs keep the children indoors all day, others take their children to parks and playgrounds, or simply for walks in the neighborhood to explore the community.

A few of the centers have television sets, which are used in a number of ways. In some centers, the children watch them only occasionally for programs such as Sesame Street, but at others, the television is the central focus of the children's day.

Similarly, centers with only a few commercially manufactured toys and few improvised playthings reflect a lack of imagination in their staffs and the likelihood of limited creative, exploratory experiences of the children. Playthings made from cans, boxes, scraps of cloth and other household items usually discarded as junk not only save money, but also demonstrate to children that they can entertain themselves happily without the things they see advertised on television. A child care center that acknowledges the limited resources of the children's parents serves families well by taking the time to show children how to use objects they might find around their own homes.

The organization of space within a children's center affects the kinds of activities conducted there. Ideally, the center should accommodate large group activities with provisions for small group or individual activities. Children need occasional respite from their playmates and should be encouraged to spend time quietly alone. Many child care providers complain of a lack of space to provide for a wide variety of simultaneous activities, but often only thoughtful reorganization of existing space can open up unforeseen possibilities and potentials. Generally, the rigid, traditional classroom arrangement seen in several of the centers may keep the children "under control," but usually at the expense of their opportunities to explore new activities and new ways of relating to playmates.

Several of the centers approach the goal of preschool preparation more formally than others, and this usually is reflected in the physical structure of the place and the ways in which adults relate to the children. Whether the adults are the focus of attention, or whether they operate on the periphery of the centers affects the type of program. Without entering into a debate between teacher-directed and child-motivated approaches to child care and developmental education, one should recognize that the physical layout of a center can either facilitate or impede the goals of the child care provider.

The attitudes of child care providers toward their responsibilities differed considerably and manifested themselves in the manner of dress, and the rapport with the children, parents and fellow workers. Since many child care directors and staffs had worked in the public school system, they continued to dress rather formally and kept children and parents at a "professional" distance. Other centers seemed much less institutionalized and much more an extension of the family. Staff members dressed in slacks or jeans and played on the floor with the children, relating as neighbors, big sisters, aunts or other relatives.

The question of bilingualism and biculturalism was approached differently by the centers. Some centers made little or no effort to incorporate the language, traditions and food of the people they served. Although some foreign-born parents welcomed the opportunity for rapid Americanization and assimilation of their children, many others wanted day care center life to more closely approximate home life. A major difference among centers serving large numbers of foreign-born families was whether they had at least one member on their staff who could speak the language of the parents and children. Surprisingly, some centers did not have even this, and had to rely on an outside interpreter for conferences with parents. Other centers had staff members and volunteer workers from the immediate community who made both parents and children feel welcome and comfortable.

The Elusive Dollar

Financial difficulties form the basis of most problems in child care. The general public has not yet fully recognized and supported the need for child care and its enormous potential for treating and preventing a wide range of social ills. Consequently, politicians have not felt the public pressure that would stir them to action. Child care appropriations sometimes are included in one social welfare or education bill or another, but rarely are funds voted in sufficient amounts and over long enough periods of time to enable child care programs to plan for long-range development and improvement. Each year, child care providers face the possibility of drastic cutbacks or new regulations by state and federal funding sources.

In addition to funding uncertainties, child care providers often find themselves involved in complicated bureaucratic processes to secure funds that already have been appropriated. Demands for strict accountability and compliance with complex local, state and federal regulations force many programs to become top-heavy with administrators, when their salaries might better be spent for teaching staff, materials and facilities.

The shortage of funds directly affects many aspects of child care programs. Obviously, it limits the quantity of supplies available for children to use, therefore limiting the developmental opportunities of the program. Overcrowded or otherwise inadequate facilities limit the amount of individual attention children receive. Many programs require full teaching credentials of their staff, but pay them less than the school system does for longer work hours and shorter vacations. Consequently, many centers report a high staff turnover rate, which denies children the opportunity to establish long-term bonds of trust and affection for child care workers.

Regulations require "active" parent and community participation in child care programs, but how it is to occur given that parents' problems managing time is usually unclear. It is talked about a lot, but seldom supported to the fullest possible degree.

Problems related to attracting and maintaining parent involvement occupy a considerable amount of child care providers' time and attention. Most working parents, especially single mothers, find that demands of managing their families and their jobs preclude their involvement in child care program activities. They recognize the vital role they can play and want their child care provider to be more responsive to their needs and expectations, but are often unable to be involved simply because of limited energy and time.

Parent involvement, however, can take many forms, all of which contribute to the success of child care programs. Parents can undertake various supportive roles, such as phone calling, fund raising, maintaining and repairing the facilities, cooking for the children, baby-sitting for the other parents in emergencies, and providing materials and supplies for the children to use.

Perhaps the most significant role parents can play lies in

policy making. The general principle that people are not committed to decisions in which they have no involvement applies directly to child care. In many cases, parental apathy originates not in a lack of interest in their children's activities, but rather in doubting that their efforts can make a difference.

Individual centers cannot be blamed entirely for poor staffing. Many directors described their efforts to find qualified staff personnel who could also speak languages other than English. The key here is the word *qualified*. State licensing requirements often include special teaching credentials, which are beyond many otherwise qualified members of ethnic or minority groups. The directors of large systems have little or no authority in selecting and hiring their staff. The criteria stress professional credentials, but do not take into consideration more subjective (and often more important) factors such as compassion, cheerfulness, love for children, warmth and energy. Many directors would like to hire their staff from the surrounding community, but are thwarted by hiring policies imposed on them by bureaucratic mandates.

Most child development specialists agree that consistency and feelings of security are among the most important needs of young children. Once assured of the love and support of at least one adult, and given a comfortable place to be (with perhaps a corner he can call his own), the child feels safe in exploring new things, testing himself in new activities with new friends. From a secure base, the child expands, develops, grows. If kept continually off-balance, wondering who cares about him and where he belongs, the child spends energy not on learning and growing, but on maintaining his equilibrium or drawing attention to his plight.

Unfortunately for many children, instability is too often a part of the child care experience. Their parents may change jobs frequently or go on and off welfare, necessitating a change in child care arrangements. Nonworking mothers often do not take their children to the child care center or home regularly. Low pay and difficult working conditions cause high staff turnover rates. As the stepchild of education and social services departments, child care programs are often shunted off to the side. In some cases, child care programs located in churches and other public buildings must share their space with other organizations, requiring daily compromises in freedom of activity. At least one child care program located in a church must virtually dismantle itself each Friday and reassemble itself on Monday to permit the church use of the space on weekends.

Child care providers, in the light of limitations on their resources and authority, often find themselves unable to meet legitimate expectations of parents. For example, many parents state that having to leave their jobs to pick up and care for their ill children imposes severe hardship on them. They expect that the child care service would make an effort to deal with common childhood ailments. A quiet area, first-aid equipment and training is basic to any children's program.

The American Academy of Pediatrics has asserted that child care providers safely can accept ill children, since by the time a child shows symptoms of an illness, he has already exposed his playmates. Once illness is accepted as an inevitability among young children, parents and child care providers can approach the problem as an integral part of the services child care should provide.

Parents complained that child care providers treated them with indifference, impatience and inconsideration. Day care providers have their own side of the story. The only opportunity many parents have to speak with the child care staff is either early in the morning or in the evening after work. These particular times are the most hectic for the staff, as children and parents are coming and going, filling the hallways and cloakrooms. Everyone — staff, parents and children — usually is tired and irritable at the beginning or end of a long day. In this rushed and impatient atmosphere, many unintended slights may occur.

Parents complain about the long waiting lists and the lack of available openings in child care programs. Child care providers sympathize with these problems, but point out that parents of children enrolled in the programs sometimes must accept part of the blame. Occasionally parents, especially those who pay little or nothing for child care, remove their children from the program without notifying the child care provider. Similarly, other parents bring their children to the centers only irregularly, or infrequently, and their children's space could go to other children in more desperate need.

Child care providers encounter conflicts as they strive to create a homelike environment. Since the children come from diverse backgrounds, the child-rearing attitudes of their parents usually differ. Parents who believe in strict discipline and unchallenged adult authority may object to child-centered programs in which children are free to choose the type and duration of their activities. In some cases, such parents prefer child care workers to dress and act like the traditional classroom teacher.

Many of the foreign-born parents, including the Latinos, Filippinos and Chinese, prefer a greater distance between their children and the child care workers, equating this with respect for adults. This contributes to creating an alien, formal and institutional environment, exactly what many child care providers try to prevent. These are the types of misunderstandings that improved communication might eliminate.

The operators of family day care homes mentioned a special problem — finding substitute caretakers when they cannot care for the children because they are ill or for other personal reasons. Many day care homes are isolated and would benefit from more pooled and shared resources. Many of these homes, however, operate without licenses and fear discovery by the authorities.

Since many of the children come from one-parent families (and that one parent is usually the mother), they most likely would benefit from contact with adult males in their child care programs. Several of the child care providers mentioned their efforts to include men on their staffs, but they also mentioned the difficulties finding either qualified or willing men. Oddly enough, several child care providers mentioned that the men on their staffs were viewed with suspicion and distrust by parents not used to seeing men work with young children.

Child care providers as a group are eager to provide the children in their care with individual attention and stimulating experiences. The lack of public awareness of their efforts, the lack of financial support by communities and governments, and the existence of outdated and ill-conceived restrictions and licensing requirements thwart the good intentions and talents of many persons active in the child care movement.

Parents: Confused, Lost, Struggling

In the study, I found that parents were having a very difficult time. The mothers included in the study were diversified as to socioeconomic status, ethnic origin, residence, marital status and number of children in the family. Typically, the mothers surveyed worked before having a child and waited sometimes two years before going back to work.

Most of the mothers had never been asked their opinions; they felt that no one had ever really been interested in their experiences. What the mothers felt they needed the most was reassurance that the child care providers cared about them and their children. They wanted a bright, cheerful place, and a loving, knowledgeable staff, willing and able to give their children individual attention. They wanted the providers to understand their difficulties and to be sensitive to them. Nine out of ten mothers expressed overwhelming difficulty in finding proper arrangements, or at being placed on long waiting lists. Transportation was often a problem in getting the children to and from the centers and homes during crowded rush hours. They felt they couldn't do their share as they usually lacked time and energy to attend the meetings. They found organizing and managing their lives with small children challenging, requiring constant scheduling.

Specific concerns related to locating good services, the child's needs and learning experiences, as well as the aspects of safety, nutrition and staff quality. Concern was also expressed over the lack of enough equipment and materials for the children.

Parents wanted their child's program to relate to and respect their cultural heritage. They wanted to know that the teachers had respect for and understood the language of their culture to the best of their ability, allowing their children to express themselves as well. The language barrier among staff, parents and children was often a problem in urban areas and a serious problem for the transmittal of cultural values.

Having the center open to coordinate with the work hours of the parents was also a difficult problem at times.

Other problems related to health and the child's well-being. Many of the mothers reported time lost from work due to their own health problems or those of their child, and described the problems of finding a program that allows children with mild illnesses to be cared for.

Mothers have come to expect that in child care, the terms reliable, inexpensive and high-quality may not be synonymous. They are lucky if they have good experiences, and want the best care they can obtain. Most parents are willing to assist in some way to improve the program, but this depends upon the staff and how they involve the parents. Parental involvement is vital to making the child care situation positive and enriching for everyone.

During the course of the investigation into child care services in San Francisco, I spoke with hundreds of parent-consumers, children, professionals, politicians, and interested citizens. Many of these people commented on what they did not like about the current system and what they would like to see improved.

Upon giving child care centers and homes a cursory glance, one at first sees smiling children, soft-spoken staff members and bustling activity. Nothing appears amiss. The children are supervised, food is provided and play encouraged. But a trained observer might note crowded and unattractive areas, little play equipment inside or out, food served in an impersonal manner, scarcity of materials and toys, staff members talking among themselves and ignoring the children or being unable to communicate with them or their parents in their language, scarcity of creative activities, lack of plants, animals or attractive decorations, poor ventilation, lack of adquate outdoor space, few record players, few musical instruments, drab bathrooms, no space for parents to sit down and talk with the staff or rest before starting home. The lack of other items then might become apparent, items such as a rocking chair, comfortable seating, an area rug, accessible bookshelves, attractive books, and other things that give a center a noninstitutional appearance and quality. Parents do not judge the center solely on the presence or lack of these items. They state as their primary concern that their child receives individual attention and affection, has opportunities for play and expanded social experiences, has nutritious, balanced and interesting food and is encouraged to try new kinds of food, receives health services and attention if needed, has an opportunity to balance his or her day with rest, learning and being able just to sit quietly and is given opportunities to gain new skills.

Parents on welfare or who have been reluctant to ask for anything else from the program simply express gratitude to have a place for their child. Parents who do not speak English find themselves frustrated when they cannot communicate with staff members who do not speak their language.

The needs and problems of the parents demonstrate the effects that poor social policy planning and services have on families. The results are a needless waste of human energy and potential. With the appropriate planning and resources, services could be improved vastly for everyone.

7 CHILD CARE ALTERNATIVES

Fortunately for the children in most communities, parents have not waited for the federal, state or local governments to act and have found alternative ways to provide care. Some of the alternatives have included child care provided by business and industry, community groups, churches, organizations, hospitals, colleges and universities and parent cooperatives.

Any child care service must maintain standards as high as possible and at least equal to minimums set for public programs. Often, because there is less red tape involved, these alternatives are more flexible and involve different kinds of groups. There are both pluses and minuses involved in setting up any child care program. The key to a good program is that everything relates to good quality in programming, from the facility to the staff and the services being provided. The basic factors involved in the physical area are site selection, building design, creation and completion of the space, installation of the physical facility and completion of the total environment. For personnel, the aspects include training and retraining, supervision, evaluation and staff development. When in operation, maintenance, financial management, catering and crisis solving are the major considerations. Schedule possibilities include full-day, part-day, night care, weekend care and drop in. The child's basic needs are education, both indoor and outdoor, and health (physical, mental and social). The child also must be seen in the context of his or her parents and the community.

When child care is seen in terms of these basic components, there is nothing mystical about the development of the services.

Because businesses are set up to make a profit, they go into a y new development with that intention and take a hard look at the costs of any program. People in the public sector often look askance at that concept, but as public programs have become more and more costly over the years, it is often difficult to ascertain where the money is being spent and what the outcomes of the programs are. A business cannot operate that way.

The range of cost can be anywhere from a thousand dollars to four thousand dollars per year, which applies to any kind of educational program. The old adage "you get what you pay for" is accurate in child care. Costs are directly related to what is provided in a given program, and it is imperative that planners determine how to meet those costs and how the program is going to function. The cost of quality programs varies even within the same city, depending on the location and the economics of what is purchased. Staff qualifications also greatly influence costs. A reduced pupil-teacher ratio is another factor. For example, if the pupil-teacher ratio is reduced from 7-1 to 4-1 the cost per child increases by approximately 42 percent. Certified teachers will double costs. An inefficiently used facility also increases the cost. A center with a capacity of 60 to 100 children can reduce costs by 10 percent. Food costs, materials, books and supplies can alter the budget, but not by much.

The basic developmental aspects for a facility involve:

Capital investment or the actual cost to create the center. This includes space per child, administrative space, construction costs, land costs or remodeling costs, equipment, supplies, taxes, etc.

Fixed operating costs include basic operations. With each new group of children the costs will vary with the total number of classrooms because of the additional teachers' salaries. The size and cost of the facility's equipment and maintenance also vary with the number of children.

Child variables will vary with the annual cost of food, medical and dental services, consumable materials and insurance. All of these factors must be analyzed by any business or group that considers going into child care.

In 1978 the number of child care centers was small compared to the national need and privately operated centers outnumbered both public and voluntary centers. Proprietary child care centers comprised 70 percent of reported services, if family child care homes were included. Quality varied from poor to excellent, costs varied from place to place and the centers operated fairly autonomously. Several of the for-profit programs that began in 1969 had very excellent ideas. They knew how to develop a cost accounting system and were able to think seriously about providing good quality services within their limitations.

Industry Interest

In March 1970, the Conference on Industry and Day Care was held in Chicago. It was open to everyone interested in thinking and learning about how industry related to child care. Many different types of business-related child care programs were discussed. These included: franchise arrangements, union company partnerships, the Amalgamated Clothing Workers of America's plan, hospital child care, small company programs and company-community programs. In addition, representatives from a model child care center called the KLH Child Development Center and the director of the Twin City area child care centers, among others, attended the conference.

It was clear that the business community was looking for direction and assistance from the federal government. Businesses were looking for guidelines, tax incentives, technical assistance, research data or assistance to develop the research they thought was needed. They wanted the cooperation of federal programs, and even wanted to provide assistance to public programs. Through a partnership with government, a great many good things might have happened. Aside from program quality concerns, the private sector offered to public programs ideas on developing cost planning, building, budgeting and cost analysis. Due to the confusion in Washington about whether child care programs were going to be supported, the much needed partnership became impossible to create at any level. A few who had that vision were not able to convince those in policy making positions of the potential impact such a partnership could make.

Children should not be franchised like hamburgers, but at the same time we should stop criticizing those who want to establish services without losing money. I do not like the idea of making profits on children, but it is impossible to justify the poor and shoddy alternatives available in too many public programs. The answer lies somewhere between the two in an efficient, cost-effective program that brings maximum benefits and operates at a cost parents and community can afford. Potentially, the possibilities of a business-government-parent partnership can make all the difference.

Many of the private programs shared ideas at this meeting. Hasbro Industries described how federal, state and local government agencies acknowledge their inability to satisfy the pressing need for child care and nursery school facilities. The work in education has been undertaken by private entrepreneurs by building schools, publishing textbooks, and manufacturing school furniture supplies and equipment.

In the development of the Romper Room Schools, Hasbro consulted with and obtained financial, legal and technical assistance. Arthur D. Little did market research with the aid of school architects and planners. The plan was to create children's services in selected communities. Plans included the conversion of the school space for community purposes when the schools were not in session, acknowledging the need to strengthen community relationships. All racial and ethnic groups of varying income levels were included in the planning of this first phase. The people were involved in site selection, construction and financing.

Another example of the business involvement in child care was the center undertaken by the telephone company in Washington, D.C. It began an experimental child care center that was located in an area that did not serve the majority of telephone company employees who could have used the center. It did not include a switchboard, referral service or other alternatives. The program did not develop in cooperation with federal programs. It asked for, but was refused, the needed assistance in establishing research criteria that would have been compatible with the concerns of the government.

With the overwhelming need for child care services, it is appalling that major utilities and government agencies could not recognize basic needs and cooperate.

Unions also have provided child care. The Amalgamated

Clothing Workers of America centers sponsored five programs in Maryland, Pennsylvania and Illinois. Child care centers were set up for employees of the departments of Labor, Health, Education and Welfare and Agriculture. In 1977 the Department of Motor Vehicles in Sacramento, California, set up a child care center for its employees.

Hospitals and Universities

More than ninety-eight hospitals in about thirty-five states operated child care centers to respond to the needs of their personnel. The entire hospital staff had used the facility, whether regularly or in an emergency. This way the hospital could maintain stability and service. For more than seven years the staff and students at the University of California Medical School fought to create a child care program. While millions were spent on research, the basic needs of the people working there went unrecognized. The plans and programs moved ahead slowly, and a center finally opened. Even doctors who were thought to be committed did little or nothing to protest the wasteful negligence and lack of concern. This story is repeated in hundreds of communities.

Having a child care center at or near a hospital is extremely important, especially if it is a teaching facility. The center may be necessary to students and faculty, and can be a special learning activity for students. In addition, the child care center provides an opportunity for giving health care to children in a way that cannot be found anywhere else. The hospital also has an opportunity to serve the community by providing health care to the general community and other child care centers and can develop specialized health care provisions for children and provide consultants to child care centers.

Services can only be provided when the employer and employee agree that a child care center is, in fact, needed, that space is available, and that it is possible to keep costs reasonable. The major reason for providing child care — aside from the importance to the company of stabilizing its work force — is that a high turnover of trained employees costs the company a great deal of money. A sensible company wants to keep a trained person rather than retrain again and again. It also would be advantageous for companies to offer part-time jobs along with part-time child care.

The advantage in having a child care center at the place of employment lies in the maintenance of a stable and productive work force. Parents can, if they want, be near their children and can, if they choose, visit them during lunch time and rest breaks and confer with or assist their teachers. Parents don't always attend the center during lunch time or snack breaks, often preferring to be with their coworkers. If parents don't become involved, it does not mean they don't care or that anything is wrong with the program. It means they are feeling assured that the children are safe and happy.

It is often illuminating for parents to observe their children through a one-way mirror and see how happy and productive they are — until the parents enter the room when the children may fuss, cry or react in other ways. This behavior is not necessarily separation anxiety; often it is simply a testing of and checking for the parent's responses. If the response is just loving, supportive and casual, the child soon learns that everything is really fine and resumes playing, forgetting about the parent.

Parents prefer an integrated work/child center, although child care at the place of employment is not always feasible for everyone. It is often difficult to bring children to the work place on crowded public transportation during rush hour. One way to solve this problem is to stagger work hours, so that people with young children come to work at a later time.

An alternative to having centers at the place of employment is to have centers in the community or on common travel routes. The Coca-Cola Company established a child care center for children of migrant employees who worked in their Florida groves. Another was located in company-sponsored housing. Another approach is to contribute to an assistance fund where money is reused for grants or loans.

Business has been involved in ways other than offering child care for profit. One way is to franchise child care. A local businessman receives a curriculum, staff pattern, budget, advertising, training and management assistance. He pays a lump sum of, perhaps, $30,000 plus a percentage of operating costs. Many businesses are franchised in this country, but not all of them have been successful. There are long hours, heavy staff costs, and many complex local regulations. Most of the time local franchisers have little experience in child care education and are just looking for a business opportunity. They do not know how complex the problems are. Keeping the costs down and enrollment up is difficult when the parents are not familiar with the program.

Another way business has been involved is in child care management. A company offers the plan, and will design and manage it for a management fee and percentage. Toy companies and other education equipment suppliers have developed services that have been used by centers.

Centers have been needed at colleges and universities throughout the country to provide for the children of students. Many women and men want to continue their education and find child care one of the most critical barriers to realizing their goals. Due to the confusing political problems, many schools that might have had programs have had difficulty securing the funding to start up. Or, once they have the programs, they have only lasted a short time. When one considers the amount of federal and state monies that support many universities, it is appalling once again to think that this very basic service — providing for children — can be that difficult and give rise to so many hundreds of meetings and discussions. Literally thousands of hours of time and energy have been spent in planning, organizing, discussing and attempting to get funding throughout the country.

The difficulties are similar all over the country. Women students and faculty wives who want to continue their study spend many hours trying to arrange for child care. Finding a good person during the day is very difficult, especially if it is only for just two or four hours. Child care is very easy for a university to provide, yet it continues to be a very difficult issue.

Child care is part of a larger political and social issue because the university can offer it to the community at large, developing both a very good program and good community relations. At Tufts College in Massachusetts, students gave $5,000 to cover the starting costs for a child care center; the student government at the University of Indiana provided $1,500 for child care; $10,000 in fees were collected at the University of Oregon; and the Student Council at the University of California in Hayward voted to allocate $7 of each student's fees to the child care center. These are just some examples of the ways in which college students have responded.

Often child care can provide compensation for the low wages that the universities pay and for the commuting that it takes to get to them. There are subsidized programs at Yale and at Syracuse, for example.

Child care can provide a wonderful opportunity for the entire campus to come together. Faculties in education, psychology, and social services can work together and involve the schools of architecture and design as both a learning and a growing experience. The possibilities are there for a great many benefits to accrue. Many see colleges and universities as having the capacity to develop low-cost, high-quality child care. An added benefit is the opportunity for student participation.

Research has many limitations but colleges and universities overcome them. The important point today is to translate the results of research and experimentation into better services for the community. The colleges and universities could provide ongoing monitoring and support systems for the child care and early childhood programs in the community, and could work to improve child care. They could offer technical assistance and provide help on budgeting and the design and development of curriculum and training.

Child care in any community is a political process, and though the politics of university child care are unique in some respects, there are lessons for nonuniversity groups interested in child care. The sources of both political and financial support are often the same. The issues always involve the nature of the center, parental control, a sliding fee scale, tuition and curriculum.

A useful book on planning a center is *How to Plan, Develop and Operate a Daycare Center*. It contains a great deal of information on operating a small cooperative center. It includes such crucial topics as finding a site, developing a classroom, planning a budget, etc., and it gives specifics.

Another book, *Designing a Daycare Center*, goes into

greater detail on creating the environment for children. It also gives descriptions and directions for setting up facilities.

Other information is provided by Educational Facilities Lab, Day Care and Child Development Council of America and other organizations listed in the Sources of Additional Information in the Appendix. A magazine called *Daycare and Early Education*, available through Human Sciences Press in New York, is another helpful source of information and resources.

Taking Responsibility

Child care continues to be an issue that has been far from resolved in our society. Certainly, if government policies encourage women to have children—or make it difficult not to have children—the nation needs to be responsible for the children that are produced.

The examples of local community groups, for example the Children's Council and Child Care Switchboard in San Francisco, can act as a guide. Their goals for 1978 were: to work for expansion of accessible publicly subsidized child care services; to cooperate with other groups and individuals to insure expansion and development of quality services for children, parents, families; to maintain a commitment to parental choice in choosing the type of child care that is suited to the family's needs; to inform and advise the general public on child care needs in San Francisco as documented by requests for services; to provide access to current regulations and legislation by publicizing and analyzing current issues and events; to promote the maintenance of standards for quality child care and developmental programs; to provide services that facilitate the active participation of parents as policy makers; to provide information and referral services to parents seeking child care and child-related services; to provide support services for the single parent; to provide technical assistance and support services to individuals and groups who provide, or wish to provide child care services with priority to those with the fewest resources; and to facilitate communication among individual agencies and organizations in order that services may be expanded through the cooperative use of existing or new resources.

Where do we go from here? How will quality child care expand in all parts of the United States? How will we provide help and encouragement to existing and potential providers of child care? How can we help parents in their efforts to find quality child care and family support services? Can we find funding for services such as a toy center, a resource center, home and center support systems and other activities?

In November 1978 Marian Wright Edelman, director of the Children's Defense Fund in Washington, D.C., issued a statement to coincide with the International Year of the Child, 1979.

> We must organize. Groups and individuals working in behalf of children must stop fighting each other and begin to build political networks across this country to educate the public and policy makers to do what is necessary for our children. We can no longer delude ourselves that children are above politics. Their lives are deeply affected by political decisions and we must become as effective as others who wield political clout.[1]

In looking at the many books and materials and reports that have been produced on child care and related areas over the years, I am reminded of the need not to lose sight of the real goals — to care for children and to let children know that we care. It is necessary to continue to expand what we are doing. We need to make sure that the best programs possible do reach the greatest number of children.

In 1959, a report by Henry Lajewski of the Children's Bureau in Washington, D.C., stated,

> Clearly the trend in our culture for the employment of mothers is part of a change so large, so strong and so rapid that we must take it into our account in our planning for children . . .
>
> How are we going to meet the problems of working parents and children? Just as we have met problems before through individuals and groups working separately and together for better community services struggling and stumbling and trying again to keep abreast with the rapid changes occurring in our culture. That is the challenge that lies ahead.

We can do no less and we can certainly do much more.[2]

8 WHAT'S NEXT?

During the past ten years, the American family has undergone a drastic transformation; whether it is for better or worse only the future can tell. The high incidence of separation and divorce creates new strains on the family, psychologically, emotionally and economically. Child care becomes an essential issue to women who return to work and must provide for themselves and their children. Without child care a woman cannot re-enter the job market or get increased training.

The availability of child care in and of itself does not weaken the family, but does address a critical need. If child care were provided early in babies' lives and mothers had frequent and supported respite from their infants or toddlers during critical times, the stress and strains that often arise in the family would be minimized. A woman's energy is often depleted after pregnancy and birth. She needs time to heal, to find some time for herself occasionally, and to pursue hobbies and interests that she had before the baby came. This does not mean she is not a good mother. In fact, she may do better for herself, her baby and her husband if she is offered the opportunity for respite. Being with a baby or toddler continuously is hard and demanding work. The strain of it can result in unconscious or conscious child abuse. Mentally or physically, the tension grows within the self and between parents. It is shortsighted not to respond to a normal, natural need among families for conveniently located child care services. It is far more advantageous to offer support early than to leave parents frustrated and not able to cope with their problems.

Dr. Urie Bronfenbrenner has written,

What is destroying the family isn't the family itself but the indifference of the rest of the society; the family takes low priority. Perhaps we need to take more seriously alternatives such as flexible work schedules, part-time jobs, convenient child care. Adults sharing of children's free time, flexible maternity leave benefits that apply to men as well as health support benefits.[1]

Families today seem to be more isolated than ever before, with insufficient support. Families need more opportunities to connect—through co-ops, switchboards, social events, and information services. For a single parent the problems are acute. Social life is curtailed, shared responsibility is sorely missed, and often the economic strain becomes crushing. Preparation for parenthood also is needed. This could occur in high schools, with education for parenthood courses and opportunities for high school boys and girls to interact in child care activities. Jobs as babysitters are important, but what is more important is that high school students learn all they can about young children.

Innovations are needed. One I envision is a child service card given to parents at the time of a child's birth. This special card would enable parents to avail themselves of services, and would be similar to a food company offering special discounts on purchases. The services would include health screening visits at the local department of health, as well as lectures, discussions, special low-cost books and materials, information on specific services in the community such as visiting nurses, plus special aid, phone numbers, nutrition information and a place to call for additional resources. Cards would be issued for different age groups, because there are definite and different needs for babies, infants, toddlers and school-age children. As a community looks at the kinds of services it offers, this card and accompanying guide could provide an enormous benefit to countless numbers of children.

Another innovation I would like to see and have been trying to create in San Francisco is a children's resource center. This is a combination of books, magazines, toys and educational materials on reserve all of the time. Not a library where books are checked out, the resource center would have a permanent collection of materials and resource people to assist parents and teachers. The resource people would be trained librarians, college students, child development specialists, retired teachers, health specialists and others who have an interest in and concern about children.

Sponsors could include state or county governments, foundations and other means of private support. The parents could make contributions based on need and use.

Another idea would involve an active and ongoing group of concerned citizens and professionals working together toward improvement of services in their own community. These child advocates would insure that programs are visited, training is available and the quality of services for children in the community meets with generally accepted standards.

Finally, I would like to see televised courses for parents, child care providers and others who work with children. The courses would cover health care, education, child growth and development, first aid, children's books, educational games and other relevant information.

Redressing the Balance

Over the past ten years, the federal government has spent enormous amounts of money for research in early childhood and child care. Much of this money has gone to colleges and universities, much of it has gone to regional laboratories, and other money has gone to contractors in consulting firms. The total amount of money spent over the past ten years in research is staggering.

I question whether this is a necessary expenditure of funds, because the balance between research and development has not been maintained. It would be far better if the colleges and universities provided services and support to their own communities. This also is true of the regional laboratories. It is hard to justify large budgets or ongoing research if the community does not benefit. It is time we stopped spending money where it does not have the biggest payoff. Children need attention and food, not data. We need to look again at the ways in which we spend money and insure that children's services get the largest piece available.

Considering the increased cutbacks in spending at all governmental levels, it becomes imperative to be realistic about the costs of child care services. An ideal solution to the problem may not be possible, but at the same time it seems criminal not to spend adequate amounts of money on children. We say we care for and want children as a matter of principle and policy. Ironically though, while professing love for children, the country's policies are influenced by certain religious groups and conservatives who want to cut off payments to poor women, and not provide abortions or follow-up care for them. If that is the case, the country must be willing to assume responsibility for the children of the more than one million teen-agers who become pregnant year year. Will the babies of these adolescents be taken care of in child care centers located in or near high schools? Will there be more cooperative linkages between the school system, the social services system, the departments of welfare and of health?

Government agencies will find that the type of conservatism that led to the adoption of Proposition 13 in California fosters cries of "we can't do anything about the problem because it's too expensive." The simple truth is that the problem requires resolution and requires it now, before another generation of children is forced to grow up unattended and neglected. Why must we produce yet another generation of abused children and then spend millions of dollars for after-the-fact research? Instead we must address the cause. The indications are, as Dr. Henry Kempe in Denver has shown, that a mother's first reactions to her baby are predictive of potential child abuse. The support is needed then, at the time of birth and delivery.

It is time to look at child care within the total system. Reading deficiencies, ill health and other problems can be solved if services are integrated within the total work and care program in each community. The time has come to stop thinking in a short-sighted way about the problems of children. It is time to look at the experiences in China and Cuba, not as rivals, but as indicators of how other societies with a total commitment are able to solve their problems. It is important to look at the systems in Canada, France, Germany, Japan, Sweden and Denmark. The United States needs to broaden its views at this time, the International Year of the Child.

It is time to put aside research and get on with action. We must feed the children and stop the study of the effects of malnutrition and neglect. It is time to utilize the results of research and make them part of the practical approaches that are used, whether in a nursery school or a day care center.

It is time to put aside the barriers that create problems, increase costs and prevent accomplishing what most needs to be done. Confronting the child care crises in this country means confronting the barriers that prevent people from being given access to employment and education. The future is our children. Our immigrant fathers came here to find a better land for us, their children. Now our children face an often hostile world, bombarded by television, advertisements, violence, noise and pollution — and they suffer for it. When parents are away from home for long periods of time and few consistent, loving surrogates are there to care, children suffer.

The educational system is a barometer of everything that is not working in our society. It is unfair to place the blame for the breakdown on that system, or welfare, the social system or the family. Unless we set aside boundaries, break down false issues, and develop workable agendas, the crisis will never be resolved. The solution is found when it is confronted. The alternatives in the community must be supported.

The Ideal Program

This country should have the finest day care centers and homes. The rich diversity of cultural and ethnic heritages adds to program capabilities. The need exists to stabilize and expand the funding sources and plan jointly for the improvement of the existing programs. Careful analysis must be made of existing centers, homes, gaps in services, and possible locations for new centers and homes. A total planning effort must be made if quality child care is to succeed. High standards, regulations, and enforcement must be built into the criteria for these programs.

The proposed child care system could provide high-quality, affordable child care services in every neighborhood for every family needing them. The services would include a wide variety of individual programs, coordinated by a broad range of social, health and educational agencies and community organizations. The system would accommodate the varying needs of current and potential child care consumers by providing full-day, half-day, drop-in, after-school and emergency evening child care services.

The city government's office of children's services would provide the focus and coordinating mechanism to mobilize government agencies and secure funds.

Existing child care programs would be improved by the expansion of health services to all children enrolled in child care centers and licensed family day care homes. Early attention to health and social problems will spare children, their families, and ultimately society the strain and expense of later remedial measures.

Every member of the community would be encouraged to contribute to this vitally needed service, including churches and other tax-exempt agencies. Parents would help plan child care services that best meet their needs and expectations. Senior citizens, high school and college students, volunteer organizations and interested individuals could be invited to spend time with children in child care arrangements, either for pay, academic credit or training, or simply personal enrichment.

A citywide children's council could receive reports on specific needs in different areas of the city from community groups.

Playgrounds and recreational services would be developed in every neighborhood to provide the opportunities for safe outdoor play that parents consistently list as one of their highest priorities.

The existing services for children must be brought together for careful assessment, evaluation, and planning at three levels: first in the office of the mayor, to secure the best possible focal point for funds and resources; second, in a community coordinating council to bring together staff and parents for each area to plan and develop the needed resources — including information, training, location of potential new sites, the improvement of existing services; third, in a community-based or district-wide consortium including representatives of the social and community service organizations in each area. In conjunction with the citywide group, all would work together both within each community and over the entire area for improvement and expansion of child care services.

The mayor's office of children's services would include representatives from education, health, recreation, social services, voluntary organizations, business and industry, mental health services, church groups and others.

The citywide coordinating council would represent each area of the city with a cross section of directors of programs, staff, parents, community organizations, family day care home operators, and health personnel.

The community child care consortium would represent within each area the directors of centers, homes, staff and parents, neighborhood organizations and religious groups to provide maximum participation in assessing needs within each community.

By extending the base of support, information and involvement, everyone concerned with the problems will have the opportunity to effect change and to participate actively in the programs. This would also maintain a system of accountability.

Child care can be improved in many other ways. Here are additional suggestions.

• Develop a program offered to junior and senior high school students which gives them the opportunity to learn about child growth and development, and provides practical experience for credit within child care programs.

• Expand the development of bilingual and bicultural experiences in all child care programs to enhance individuality and uniqueness, and to stress the contributions made by all ethnic groups. Improve the ability of the staff to plan and communicate with children and parents. Provide ethnic foods within the basic diet offered at the centers and homes.

• Include developmentally disabled children in the child care centers and offer special training to the staff to meet the needs of these children and their families.

• Improve the physical facilities of every child care center and home in the city to provide adequate play space and playground equipment at, or accessible to, the program.

• Provide emergency twenty-four-hour care where the need is greatest. Work shifts, family problems or sudden illness should not result in undue hardship on children. A program that offers support to the family under stress benefits children in the long run.

• Require a fully maintained first-aid kit and certification of several staff persons in basic essentials of emergency care within each program.

- Develop systematic record keeping for children in all programs so that essential information with regard to education and health be available to follow the child throughout his or her schooling.
- Provide for the care of infants within small centers or homes. This should be accessible to other services, such as programs for older children in the same family.
- Develop a system of family day care home support by connecting centers and homes. This could improve the services provided by each, supply materials and staff, and give the city an immediate expanded child care system.
- Develop a child care resource materials and consultation service with accessible publications and information to assist people as they plan and implement their programs.
- Secure space in every public housing project for child care services. Care should also be provided in hospitals, clinics, and other public buildings.
- Develop an informal newsletter for interested persons within programs and in the community to publicize new developments, information, and provide a way of learning about additional services.
- Offer flexible training programs to directors, staff and family day care home operators to sensitize them to the special developmental needs of young children.
- Plan a comprehensive health care delivery system so all children will receive diagnostic services, screening and health maintenance as they require it. Hospitals and health departments should be responsible for drawing up plans that will reach the largest number of children in all child care programs in the city.
- Maintain liaison between child advocates in the community and Washington to bring current and proposed plans to the attention of legislators and program developers, and to obtain the necessary funds to carry out the required services.
- Assess current regulations governing buildings and facilities for centers and homes, as well as reasons for the delay in obtaining licensed facilities. Funds should be allocated or secured for the improvement of existing programs. Usable space should be

brought to the attention of the agencies or organizations involved so new services can be developed.

• Improve communication for parents seeking child care, drop-in care, half-, full-day or specialized services. Give attention to the problems of non-English-speaking parents to lessen the frustrations in their attempts to secure child care.

• Expand current after-school programs by providing a comprehensive before- and after-school service in every school. This can be accomplished on a city and neighborhood basis by having a responsive series of activities planned and supervised. The program would include scouts, a neighborhood arts council, voluntary organizations, senior citizens and others, including teens and college students.

• Encourage industry-supported child care for employees. The centers can be developed at or near the place of employment, or by contributions made to the child care programs already in existence.

• Encourage churches and other tax-exempt institutions to provide existing space free or at nominal rental fees for child care programs.

By working together, people who care can make an enormous contribution toward insuring that future generations attain their fullest potential and become responsible, economically independent members of society. Unless we pay attention and are willing to work together to resolve many of the issues and lift the barriers to overcome them, the child care crisis will continue to confront us.

APPENDICES

Sources of Additional Information about Child Care and Programs for Children

Agency for Children, Youth and Families
U.S. Department of Health, Education and Welfare
Box 1182
Washington, DC 20013

American Academy of Pediatrics
P.O. Box 1037
Evanston, IL 60204

American Home Economics Association
2010 Massachusetts Avenue, NW
Washington, DC 20016

American Nurses Association
2420 Pershing Road
Kansas City, MO 64108
or
1030 15th Street, NW
Washington, DC 20005

American Psychological Association
1947 Rosemary Hills Drive
Silver Springs, MD 20910

Appalachian Regional Commission
1666 Connecticut Avenue, NW
Washington, DC 20235

Association for Childhood Education International
3615 Wisconsin Avenue, NW
Washington, DC 20016

Bank Street College of Education
69 Bank Street
New York, NY 10014

Black Child Development Institute
1028 Connecticut Avenue, NW
Washington, DC 20036

Child Development Associate Consortium
805 15th Street
Suite 500
Washington, DC 20005

Child Study Association of America
9 East 89th Street
New York, NY 10028

Child Welfare League of America
67 Irving Place
New York, NY 10003

Children's Defense Fund
1763 R Street, NW
Washington, DC 20009

Coalition for Children and Youth
191 K Street, NW
Washington, DC 20006

Council on Social Work Education
345 East 46th Street
New York, NY 10017

Day Care and Child Development Council of America
Suite 1100
1401 K Street, NW
Washington, DC 20005

Educational Facilities Laboratory
477 Madison Avenue
New York, NY 10022

Educational Resources Childhood Education Information Center (ERIC)
Clearinghouse on Early
University of Illinois
805 West Pennsylvania Avenue
Urbana, IL 61801

Government Printing Office
Washington, DC 20402
(Many documents published by various
government agencies and departments can
be obtained directly from the GPO.)

National Association for the Education
of Young Children
1834 Connecticut Avenue, NW
Washington, DC 20009

National Council of Organizations
for Children and Youth
1910 K Street, NW
Washington, DC 20006

National Education Association
1201 16th Street, NW
Washington, DC 20036

National Federation of Settlements
and Neighborhood Centers
232 Madison Avenue
New York, NY 10016

National Association of Social Workers
20 E Street, NW
Washington, DC 20001

National League for Nursing
10 Columbus Circle
New York, NY 10023

United States Office of Education
Department of Health, Education
and Welfare
Washington, DC 20201

Women's Bureau
United States Department of Labor
Washington, DC 20201

Veto message of Richard M. Nixon, December 9, 1971

Office of the White House Press Secretary

THE WHITE HOUSE

TO THE SENATE OF THE UNITED STATES.

I return herewith without my approval S. 2007, the Economic Opportunity Amendments of 1971.

This legislation undertakes three major Federal commitments in the field of social welfare: extension of the Economic Opportunity Act of 1964, creation of a National Legal Services Corporation, and establishment of a comprehensive child development program . . .

But the most deeply flawed provision of this legislation is Title V, "Child Development Programs."

Adopted as an amendment to the OEO legislation, this program points far beyond what this administration envisioned when it made a "national commitment to providing all American children an opportunity for a healthful and stimulating development during the first five years of life."

Though Title V's stated purpose, to provide every child with a full and fair opportunity to reach his full potential, is certainly laudable, the intent of Title V is overshadowed by the fiscal irresponsibility, administrative unworkability, and family weakening implications of the system it envisions. We owe our children something more than good intentions.

We cannot and will not ignore the challenge to do more for America's children in their all-important early years. But our response to this challenge must be a measured, evolutionary, painstakingly considered one, consciously designed to cement the family in its rightful position as the keystone of our civilization.

Further, in returning this legislation to the Congress, I do not for a moment overlook the fact that there are some needs to be served, and served now.

One of these needs is for day care, to enable mothers, particularly those at the lowest income levels, to take full time jobs. Federal support for State and local day care services under Head Start and the Social Security Act already totals more than half a billion dollars a year — but this is not enough. That is why our H.R. 1 welfare reform proposals, which have been before the Congress for the past twenty-six months, include a request for $750 million annually in day care funds for welfare recipients and the working poor, including $50 million for construction of facilities.

And that is why we support the increased tax deductions written into the Revenue Act of 1971, which will provide a significant Federal subsidy for day care in families where both parents are employed, potentially benefiting 97 percent of all such families in the country and offering parents free choice of the child care arrangements they deem best for their own families. This approach reflects my conviction that the Federal Government's role wherever possible should be one of assisting parents to purchase needed day care services in the private, open market, with Federal involvement in direct provision of such services kept to an absolute minimum.

A second imperative is the protection of children from actual suffering and deprivation. The administration is already moving on this front, under a policy of concentrating assistance where it will help the most is a policy certain to suffer if Title V's scattering of attention and resources were to become law. Action we are presently taking includes:

Expansion of nutritional assistance to poor children by nearly tripling participation in the food stamp program (from 3.6 million people to 10.6 million people) and doubling support for child nutrition programs (from less than $600 million to more than $1.2 billion) since 1969;

Improvement of medical care for poor children through the introduction of more vigorous screening and treatment procedures under Medicaid;

More effective targeting of material and child health services on low income mothers who need them most.

Furthermore, Head Start continues to perform both valuable day care and early education services, and an important experimentation and demonstration function which identifies and paves the way for wider application of successful techniques. And the Office of Child Development which I established within the Department of Health, Education and Welfare in 1969 provides overall leadership for these and many other activities focused on the first five years of life.

But, unlike these tried and tested programs for our children, the child development envisioned in this legislation would be truly a long leap into the dark for the United States Government and the American people. I must share the view of those of its supporters who proclaim this to be the most radical piece of legislation to emerge from the Ninety-second Congress.

I also hold the conviction that such far-reaching national legislation should not, must not, be enacted in the absence of a great national debate upon its merit, and broad public acceptance of its principles.

Few contend that such a national debate has taken place. No one, I believe, would contend that the American people, as a whole, have

determined that this is the direction in which they desire their government and nation to go.

Specifically, these are my present objections to the proposed child
development program:

First, neither the immediate *need* nor the desirability of a national
child development program of this character has been demonstrated.

Secondly, day care centers to provide for the children of the poor so
that their parents can leave the welfare rolls to go on the payrolls of the
nation, are already provided for in H.R. 1, my workfare legislation. To
some degree, child development centers are a duplication of these efforts.
Further, these child development programs would be redundant in that
they duplicate many existing and growing Federal, State and local efforts
to provide social, medical, nutritional and educational services to the very
young.

Third, given the limited resources of the Federal budget, and the
growing demands upon the Federal taxpayers, the expenditure of two
billions of dollars in a program whose effectiveness has yet to be demonstrated cannot be justified. And the prospect of costs which would
eventually reach $20 billion annually is even more unreasonable.

Fourth, for more than two years this administration has been
working for the enactment of welfare reform, one of the objectives of
which is to bring the family together. This child development program
appears to move in precisely the opposite direction. There is a respectable
school of opinion that this legislation would lead toward *altering the* family
relationship. Before even a tentative step is made in this direction by their
government, the American people should be fully consulted.

Fifth, all other factors being equal, good public policy requires that
we enhance rather than diminish both parental authority and parental
involvement with children — particularly in those decisive early years
when social attitudes and a conscience are formed, and religious and moral
principles are first inculcated.

Sixth, there has yet to be an adequate answer provided to the
crucial question of who the qualified people are, and where they would
come from, to staff the child development centers.

Seventh, as currently written, the legislation would create, ex
nihilo, a new army of bureaucrats. By making any community over 5,000
population eligible as a direct grantee of HEW child development funds,
the proposal actively invites the participation of as many as 7,000 prime
sponsors — each with its own plan, its own council, its own version of all
the other machinery that has made Head Start, with fewer than 1,200
grantees, so difficult a management problem . . .

Eighth, the States would be relocated to an insignificant role. This cation to the Federal Government from the States — only eight of which even require kindergarten at present. It would also retain an excessive new program would not only arrogate the initiative for preschool edu-measure of operational control for such education at the Federal level, in the form of the standards and program guidelines to be set down by the Secretary of HEW.

Ninth, for the Federal Government to plunge headlong financially into supporting child development would commit the vast moral authority of the National Government to the side of communal approaches to child rearing over against the family-centered approach.

This President, this Government, is unwilling to take that step. With this message, I urge the Congress to act now to pass the OEO extension and to create the legal services corporation along the lines proposed in our original legislation.

Statement of Walter Mondale

While he was in the Senate, Vice President Walter Mondale was a tireless worker for child care legislation. In a contribution to a book entitled Toward a Responsible Presidency, *published in 1975, then-Senator Mondale described how child care legislation was sabotaged by the Nixon Administration.*

During the Nixon Presidency, virtually every member of the Congress, at some point, experienced the frustration created by the lack of accountability in the White House. Policy decisions were centralized there, the Congress was almost totally excluded from any consultative processes, and Cabinet officers and their departments in most areas were often left without independent authority. The process became predictable. Two examples are illustrative of the Nixon White House style.

For over five years, I have been working for enactment of a Child Development Act to provide, on a voluntary basis, quality child care to the millions of American children whose parents are working or for children deeply affected by poverty. In 1971, those of us supporting this legislation conducted weeks of negotiations with then Health, Education and Welfare Secretary Elliot Richardson. The Secretary met with House and Senate conferees working on a final version of this legislation in late 1971. After a lengthy discussion, we agreed that the conferees would modify the bill under consideration and submit the modifications to him for comments. We did so, and he replied favorably regarding the revised version. Encouraged by this reply, the conference tentatively adopted the revised version and sent it to the Secretary for his official comments. When he suggested further modifications, we acceded to them and he indicated that he supported the revised bill and would do everything possible to get the President to sign it.

We felt that a compromise had been worked out in good faith which met the main objections of the administration while not violating the central purposes of the legislation. We thought we had an understanding, so on November 15 the conferees met for the final session, ratified this understanding, agreed to file the conference report, and adjourned the conference. But one week later, Senator Gaylord Nelson, chairman of the conference, received a letter from Secretary Richardson, dated November 18, in which the Secretary indicated quite clearly that he was no longer supporting this bill, regardless of our understanding.

Without ever mentioning the issues we had negotiated or the agreements we had reached, Secretary Richardson's letter suggested that he had misunderstood other provisions in the bill agreed to in conference and made it clear that the other provisions were unacceptable to him.

We may never know for sure why Secretary Richardson changed his mind, wrote that letter, and decided not to support the bill as he had previously agreed. But the general feeling in Congress was that Secretary Richardson did support the bill, went to the White House and urged that the bill be signed, and lost that argument to the people who ran the Domestic Council.

Predictably, on December 9, 1971, President Nixon vetoed the Child Development Act and now four years later, millions of children in this nation are still without the decent child care they so desperately need and deserve.

In one week, anonymous, unaccountable White House aides had reversed the work of Senate and House conferees dealing directly with the Cabinet Secretary whose responsibility it was to represent the administration position.

Similarly, in 1972, Secretary Richardson negotiated a compromise version of the Nixon administration's Family Assistance Plan with Senator Abraham Ribicoff of Connecticut. The compromise was agreed to and announced publicly, and the Secretary stated that he would go to the President and attempt to get him to help rally the Republican support necessary to get a bill adopted by the Senate. Shortly thereafter, the President stated that the compromise version reached by the Secretary with the Senate was unacceptable and that either the House version of this legislation was passed or a veto would follow. The practical and predictable result of this action was that no family assistance bill passed the Senate, thus no conference was possible and no bill could be enacted. Once again, the will of the Congress and the Cabinet had been thwarted by a White House staff accountable only to the President.

To me, these will always be examples of how Cabinet members, in the Nixon years, did not have the authority to negotiate with the Congress, and if they did negotiate and reach agreement, those agreements could be, and often were, reversed by the Domestic Council and the White House staff.

These were merely two instances of how policy was made during the Nixon years. The pattern was clear for all to see. As members of Congress, we worked on a particular piece of legislation with the appropriate Cabinet officer, believing that he should be the person representing the administration, since he was subject to Senate confirmation and general congressional oversight. Yet we found out that Robert Finch or Elliot Richardson or Claude Brinegar were often not in a position to make real commitments.

This, in turn, prevented the essential political and legislative process of give and take between the Congress and the administration from ever occurring in a meaningful way, and produced more vetoes and more misunderstanding than was necessary or desirable.

Statement of the National Women's Conference
National Plan of Action
Houston, Texas, November 18-21, 1977

Following the Nixon, and later the Ford, veto and the general reduction or dismantling of the programs and coordination of service efforts, the state of child care needs in the United States was reflected again by the statement developed for the National Plan of Action, National Women's Conference in Houston, Texas.

The statement and background were presented to the conference and approved unanimously.

The Federal government should assume a major role in directing and providing comprehensive, voluntary, flexible hour, bias-free, non-sexist, quality child care and developmental programs, including child care facilities for Federal employees, and should request and support adequate legislation and funding for these programs.

Federally funded child care and developmental programs should have low-cost, ability-to-pay fee schedules that make these services accessible to all who need them, regardless of income, and should provide for parent participation in their operation.

Legislation should make special provision for child care facilities for rural and migrant worker families.

Labor and management should be encouraged to negotiate child care programs in their collective bargaining agreements.

Education for parenthood programs should be improved and ex-panded by local and State school boards, with technical assistance and experimental programs provided by the Federal government.

City, county and/or State networks should be established to provide parents with hotline consumer information on child care, referrals, and follow-up evaluations of all listed care givers.

Summary Background:

The majority of American mothers of school-age children are now in the labor force. More than six million children under six have working mothers, and at least 4.6 million have mothers who are single, separated, divorced or widowed heads of families. At least 18,000 children under six are caring for themselves during the work day. Another 1.8 million children seven to thirteen years old take care of themselves until one of their parents returns from work.

There are only limited numbers of day care centers supported by private industry, unions and businesses for children of employees. The Federal government funds child care programs chiefly as tools to move low-income mothers off public assistance, rather than as safe and healthy learning experiences for children with working parents of diverse incomes. Middle-income parents are too often excluded from publicly funded programs as are parents who work only part-time or on a voluntary basis or attend school and need only part-time or irregular child care for their families.

The working parent's search for convenient, affordable, dependable quality child care is often lonely, desperate and conducted under pressure of a deadline. Even where there are central registries of child care providers, evaluations of these providers are not commonly available.

Most training for care providers does not now meet the need for programs in which children are not sex stereotyped, or in which disabled children as well as all racial, ethnic and social groups are served.

Statement of Senator Alan Cranston

California Senator Alan Cranston has introduced legislation designed to shape a child care system. Following are excerpted remarks he made when introducing his bill.

Mr. President, the Subcommitte on Child and Human Development, which I am privileged to chair, recently completed a series of four hearings on the subject of child-care and child-development programs. The purpose of these hearings was to solicit the comments of parents, child-care providers, and others concerned with the welfare of children about the need for Federal legislation in the child-care area and how best to shape such legislation . . .

The need for adequate child-care services in this country has been documented time and again. Statistics released by the U.S. Department of Labor in March of 1977 indicate that a majority — 51 percent — of the mothers of children under the age of eighteen work outside of the home. Most of these working mothers have entered the labor force for reasons of financial necessity, and two-thirds work full time. These statistics also indicate that 41 percent of the mothers with children under the age of six are in the labor force.

In the terms of the numbers of children involved, these statistics translate to 6.4 million children under the age of 6 whose mothers work and 22.4 million children from 6 to 17 whose mothers work. Yet, there are only 1.6 million licensed child-care openings, including center-based and family-based child care, available throughout the Nation, according to 1976 data from HEW — enough to cover only 25 percent of the children under 6 whose mothers work. Many witnesses at our hearing concluded from this data that substantial numbers of children are left in inadequate care, shuffled from one care arrangement to another, or simply left alone while the mother is at work . . .

Although the need for more child care seems clear, the solution has not been easy to come by. Several attempts have been made in Congress over the last 8 years to enact comprehensive child-care legislation. In 1971, we passed such a bill, but it was vetoed by President Nixon. In 1975, hearings were held in both Houses of Congress on similar legislation, the proposed Child and Family Services Act, introduced by former Senator Mondale and Congressman Brademas, but no action was taken on that legislation in either body.

Today, it appears that the need for child-care legislation is even greater than it was 8 years ago. Although the Federal Government already provides support — either directly through social services programs funded through Title XX of the Social Security Act which are targeted toward welfare recipients and poor families, or indirectly through tax credits which benefit primarily middle- and upper-income families — large numbers of low-income, working families receive little or no assistance from these programs. Many families, struggling to stay in the work force and off welfare, are simply unable to find reasonable quality child care at prices they can afford in the present marketplace. Some families are able to find neighbors or relatives to take care of the children — and many of these arrangements are adequate. Many others, however, are forced to leave their children alone or in unsafe or unhealthy situations . . .

Mr. President, many who testified stressed the fact that most women work for the same reasons that men do: financial necessity. Their incomes may be the only one the family has — as with the 9.7 million single parents in this country — or their income may make the difference between poverty and a decent living. Marian Wright Edelman, director of the Children's Defense Fund, noted in her testimony to the subcommittee that in 1974 almost 2 million families with incomes over $5,000 were kept there by the wife's income and that 4.5 million families with earnings over $10,000 were kept above the poverty line by the wife's income. According to Ms. Edelman, in single parent families headed by women, the average income is $7,513 if the mother works and $3,794 if she does not . . .

Finally, Mr. President, most of the witnesses noted that parental involvement is related to quality in a number of ways. First, there was a feeling that parents are good arbitrators of quality in child-care programs. One witness noted that a parent can almost always tell whether a child wants to go back to the program and that this is, in itself, a good indicator of quality. Several witnesses said that parents should be involved in setting standards for licensing and in monitoring programs for compliance. Nearly all agreed that it was important to involve parents in the process of planning to meet child-care needs . . .

Mr. President, I want to emphasize that the legislation I am proposing would in no way interfere with the role and responsibilities of parents in raising and caring for their children. The family is and must continue to be the primary influence upon children, and it is absolutely critical that any Federal legislation proposed recognize — and, indeed, reinforce — this principle. The legislation I am proposing will make assistance available to parents who request help in finding child care for their chidlren while they work to support their families. I think it is important to stress that participation in any of the child-care programs supported by this legislation would be strictly at the option of the parent.

It is not intended to, nor will it, set up governmental agencies or anyone else to intervene in any of the decisions parents make about how they want to rear their chidlren, nor will it provide any agencies — public or private — with any basis for interfering with child-rearing decisions parents may make.

Mr. President, both by making it absolutely clear that participation in any program supported by this legislation is totally voluntary, and by providing parents who seek assistance the right to choose among a variety of options the type of child care they want for their children, as well as providing for meaningful roles for parents in the setting of policy and planning for child-care programs at the local and State levels, I believe we make it truly possible for parents to make the decisions and choices about how they want their children cared for while they work.

Mr. President, I also want to stress the fact that by providing additional Federal assistance for families in need of child-care services for their children, we are providing the kind of assistance which holds families together. The testimony presented at our hearings describing children being separated from their parents and sent to other States to live when child care was not available in their community provides a dramatic illustration of how families can actually be broken up when adequate child care is not available. The incredible stress and strains placed upon working parents when they are unable to find reliable child care also contribute to family disintegration. Child care services for families that need them both support families and help them to function and stay together . . .

Mr. President, I hope that this legislation will be received by all those interested in this area as a new beginning toward enactment of comprehensive child-care legislation. I also hope that a constructive dialogue will be stimulated around this legislation so that our goals can be achieved in the foreseeable future.

NOTES

CHAPTER ONE: WHO NEEDS CHILD CARE?

1. National Research Council, "The State of American Families and Children," *Toward A National Policy for Children and Family* (Washington, D.C.: National Academy of Science, 1976), p. 14.
2. James Hymes, "Child Care Problems of the Night Shift Mother," *Journal of Consulting Psychology* VIII (November 1944): 225-228.
3. Bernard Greenblatt, *Responsibility for Child Care* (San Francisco: Jossey-Bass), p. 64.
4. Selma Fraiberg, *Every Child's Birthright: In Defense of Mothering* (New York: Basic Books, 1977), p. 45.
5. Richard M. Nixon, Veto Message. See Appendix.
6. Gilbert Steiner with Pauline H. Milius, *The Children's Cause* (Washington, D.C.: The Brookings Institution, 1976), p. 251.
7. Pamela Roby, *Child Care: Who Cares?* (New York: Basic Books, 1973), p. 6.
8. Mary Keyserling, *Windows on Day Care* (New York: National Council of Jewish Women, 1972), p. 18.
9. Lorraine Keiman and James Jekel, *School Age Mothers' Problems, Programs and Policy* (Hamden, Conn.: Shoe String Press), p. 3.
10. National Academy of Sciences, Toward a National Policy for Children and Family, National Academy of Sciences, Washington, DC, 1976, pp. 14-15.

CHAPTER TWO: DON'T FORGET THE PARENTS

1. Margaret Mead, "Statement of Principles in Day Care," p. 3; *New Realities*, p. 37.
2. "Statement of Principles in Day Care," (Washington, D.C.: Office of Child Development, HEW, 1972).
3. Florence Ruderman, *Child Care and Working Mothers*, Child Welfare Council, pp. 6-10.
4. Woods, "The Unsupervised Child of the Working Mother," *Developmental Psychology* (Washington, D.C.: The American Psychological Association, 1972).
5. Sally Wenkdos Olds, *The Mother Who Works Outside the Home*, Child Study Association, p. 11.

CHAPTER FOUR: THE STATE OF THE STATES

1. Wilson Riles, *Commission on Child Care and Development Services Report*, State Department of Education, 1978.
2. *America's Children*, National Council of Organizations for Children and Youth (Washington, D.C., 1976).
3. Education Commission of the States, *Compact* (Denver, Colo.) December 1969, pp. 20-24.
4. Ibid., p. 25.
5. Ibid., p. 27.
6. Gilbert Steiner, *Policies and Politics in Child Welfare* (New York: Brookings Institution), p. 4.
7. James Gallagher, *Compact*, Education Commission of the States, p. 20
8. Education of the States, *Report on Early Childhood*, 1971, p. 20.

CHAPTER FIVE: MAKING IT WORK ON THE LOCAL LEVEL

1. Bettye Caldwell, "Can Young Children Have a Quality Life in Day Care?" *Young Children*, 28 April 1973.
2. James A. Levine, *Day Care in the Public Schools — Profiles of Five Communities* (Cambridge, Mass.: Education Development Center, 1978) p. 29.
3. Ibid., p. 128.

CHAPTER SEVEN: CHILD CARE ALTERNATIVES

1 Marian Wright Edelman, *Young Children*, November 1978, p. 3.
2. Child Care Arrangements of Full-Time Working Mothers, Children's Bureau, United States Department of Health, Education and Welfare, Washington, DC, 1959, p. iii.

CHAPTER EIGHT: WHAT'S NEXT?

1. Urie Bronfenbrenner, *Psychology Today*, May 1978.

BIBLIOGRAPHY

Other Publications by the Author

Auerbach, Stevanne, ed. *Child Care: A Comprehensive Guide*. New York Human Sciences Press, 1975-1979. 4 vols. Vol. 1, Rationale for Child Care Services Programs U.S. Politics. Vol. 2, Model Programs and Their Components. Vol. 3, Creative Centers and Homes. Vol. 4, Special Needs and Services.

———. "Child Care: A Cruel Hoax." *The Humanist*, vol. 32, December 1972.

———. "Child Care in the Workplace." *Humanizing the Workplace*. Buffalo: Prometheus Books, 1974.

———. "Child Care Services: Should the Public Provide Them?" *Phi Delta Kappa*, vol. 57, April 1976.

———. "The Children are Waiting." 30-minute TV Documentary. KQED, Channel 9, San Francisco, April 1974.

———, and Freedman, Linda. *Choosing Child Care: A Guide for Parents*. Published by Parents and Child Care Resources in cooperation with the Far West Laboratory for Educational Research and Development. Institute for Childhood Resources, 1976.

———. "Day Care: The Forgotten Priority." *National Elementary Principal*, vol. 55, July-August 1976.

———. "Federally Sponsored Child Care." In *Child Care: Who Cares? Foreign and Domestic Infant and Early Childhood Development Policies*, edited by Pamela Roby. New York: Basic Books, 1973.

———. "Mothers' Expectations of Child Care." *Young Children*, May 1977.

———. *The Need for Day Care for the Children of Federal Employees*. Testimony presented to the Select Subcommittee on Education and Labor, John Brademas, Chairman; in Hearings on Child Care H.R. 13520 Comprehensive Preschool Education and the Child Care Act of 1969. Washington, D.C., December 16, 1969.

———. *Parents and Child Care — A Report on Child Care Consumers in San Francisco: A Study of Parental Expectations for Child Care Services from a Cross-Cultural Perspective*. San Francisco: Far West Laboratory for Educational Research and Development, 1974.

———. "Unmet Needs in Child Care." *San Francisco Magazine*, vol. 17, June 1976.

———. "What Mothers Want from Child Care." *Day Care and Early Childhood*, vol. 1, April 1974.

———. *The Whole Child Catalog: A Sourcebook for Parents*. New York: G.P. Putnam's Sons, 1979.

Other Publications

Chapter One: Who Needs Child Care?

Curtis, Jean. *Working Mothers*. Garden City, N.Y.: Doubleday, 1976.

Fraiberg, Selma. *Every Child's Birthright: In Defense of Mothering*. New York: Basic Books, 1977.

Gilder, George F. "The Case Against Universal Day Care." *The New Leader*, April 3, 1972.

Harrell, James A. *Selected Readings in the Issues of Day Care*. Washington, D.C.: The Day Care and Child Development Council of America, Inc., 1972.

Hoffman, Lois Wladis, and Nye, F. Ivan. *Working Mothers*. San Francisco: Jossey-Bass Publishers, 1974.

Howell, Mary C. *Helping Ourselves: Families and the Human Network*. Boston: Beacon Press, 1975.

Joffe, Carole E. *Friendly Intruders: Child Care Professionals and Family Life*. Berkeley: University of California Press, 1977.

Kenniston, Kenneth, and the Carnegie Council on Children. *All Our Children: The American Family Under Pressure*. New York: First Harvest/HBJ, 1978.

Keyserling, Mary Dublin. *Windows on Day Care*. New York: National Council of Jewish Women, 1972.

Levine, James A. *Who Will Raise the Children? New Options for Fathers (and Mothers)*. New York: Lippincott, 1976.

Levitan, Sar A., and Alderman, Karen Cleary. *Child Care & ABC's Too*. Baltimore and London: The Johns Hopkins University Press, 1975.

Resources for Community Change. *Demand for Day Care: An Introduction for Campus and Community*. Washington, D.C.: Day Care and Child Development Council, 1974.

Roby, Pamela. *Child Care — Who Cares?* New York: Basic Books, 1973.

Sidel, Ruth. *Women and Child Care in China: A Firsthand Report*. New York: Hill and Wang, 1972.

Steinfels, Margaret O'Brien. *Who's Minding the Children? The History and Politics of Day Care in America*. New York: Simon and Schuster, 1973.

Chapter Four: The State of the States

Adair, Thelman, and Eckstein, Esther. *Parents and the Day Care Center*. New York: Federation of Protestant Welfare Agencies, 1969.

Andrews, J.D., ed. *One Child Indivisible*. Washington, D.C.: The National Association for the Education of America, 1970.

Boguslawski, Dorothy Beers. *Guide for Establishing and Operating Day Care Centers for Young Children.* New York: Child Welfare League of America, 1970.

Caldwell, Bettye M. "Can Young Children Have a Quality Life in Day Care?" *Young Children, April 1973. Reprint.*

———. *"A Timid Giant Grows Bolder." Saturday Review,* February 20, 1971.

———. "The Effects of Infant Care." *Review of Child Development Research,* vol. 1. New York: Russell Sage Foundation, 1964.

Cohen, Monroe D., ed. *Help for Day Care Workers.* Reprint from *Childhood Education.* Washington, D.C.: Association of Social Workers, 1976.

Collins, Alice H., and Pancoast, Diane L. *Natural Helping Networks: A Strategy for Prevention.* Washington, D.C.: National Association of Social Workers, 1976.

Commission on the Status of Women. "Steps in Setting Up A Child Care Center." State of California, March 1975.

Day Care Council of New York. *So You're Going to Run a Day Care Service.* New York, Autumn 1971.

Evans, E. Belle; Saia, George; and Evans, Elmer A. *Designing a Day Care Center.* Boston: Beacon Press, 1974.

Evans, E. Belle; Shub, Beth; and Weinstein, Marlene. *Day Care: How To Plan, Develop and Operate a Day Care Center.* Boston: Beacon Press, 1971.

Griffin, Al. *How to Start and Operate a Day Care Home.* Chicago: Henry Regnery Co., 1973.

LeLaurin, Kathryn, and Risley, Todd R. "The Organization of Day Care Environments: The 'Zone Defense' versus the 'Man-to-Man Defense.' " *Journal of Applied Behavior Analysis,* September 5, 1971.

National Association for Community Development, The. *Early Childhood Development: Outlook for 1970.* Washington, D.C., January 1970.

National Research Council, The. *Toward a National Policy for Children and Families.* Washington, D.C.: National Academy of Sciences, 1976.

Osmon, Fred Linn. *Patterns for Designing Children's Centers.* New York: Educational Facilities Laboratories, 1971.

Prescott, Elizabeth. "The Large Day Care Center as a Child-Rearing Environment." *Voice for Children,* vol. 2. 1971.

Prescott, Elizabeth; Milich, Cynthia; and Jones, Elizabeth. *The "Politics" of Day Care,* vol. 1. Washington, D.C.: National Association for the Education of Young Children, 1972.

Provence, Sally; Naylor, Audrey; and Patterson, June. *The Challenge of Day Care.* New Haven and London: Yale University Press, 1977.

Sale, June S., and Torres, Yolanda L. *"I'm Not Just A Babysitter": A Descriptive Report of the Community Family Day Care Project.* Reprinted by The Day Care and Child Development Council of America, 1972.

Shannon, William. "A Radical, Direct, Simple, Utopian Alternative to Day-Care Centers." *New York Times Magazine*, April 30, 1972.

Shapiro, Carol. *How to Organize a Child Care Center*. New York: Women's Action Alliance, 1973.

Yankelovic, Skelly and White. *Raising Children in a Changing Society*. The General Mills American Family Report, Battle Creek, Mich. 1976-1977.

Chapter Five: Making It Work on the Local Level

Class, Norris E. *Public Policy and Working Mothers: A Historical Analysis of the American Experience*. Washington, D.C.: Department of Health, Education and Welfare, Office of Child Development, June 22, 1972.

Grotberg, Edith. *A Review of the Present Status and Future Needs in Day Care Research. A Working Paper*. Washington, D.C.: Office of Child Development, November 1971.

Keyserling, Mary Dublin. "Washington Social Legislation Bulletin." *Social Legislation Information Service*, vol. 25, September 25, 1978.

Markuson, Stan. *Special WIN Child Care Report* (AUER–1628–TR–3002). Philadelphia: Auerbach Corporation, March 15, 1970.

National Council of Organizations for Children and Youth. *America's Children 1976. A Bicentennial Assessment*. Washington, D.C., 1976.

National Research Council. *Toward a National Policy for Children and Family*. Washington, D.C.: National Academy of Sciences, 1976.

Mayer, Anna B., with the collaboration of Kahn, Alfred J. *Day Care as a Social Instrument*. New York: Columbia University School of Social Work, January 1965. Mimeographed.

Office of the Assistant Secretary for Education. *Federal Policy for Preschool Services: Assumptions and Evidence*. Menlo Park, Calif.: Stanford Research Institute, May 1975.

Office of the Assistant Secretary for Planning and Evaluation. *Policy Issues in Day Care: Summaries of 21 Papers*. Washington, D.C.: Department of Health, Education and Welfare, November 1977.

Office of Child Development. *Day Care: A Statement of Principles* (Publication No. OCD 73-2). Washington, D.C.: Department of Health, Education and Welfare, July 1970.

Office of Human Development. Office of Child Development. Head Start Bureau, Head Start. *Statistical Highlights from the National Child Care Consumer Study*. Washington, D.C.: Department of Health, Education and Welfare, 1976.

Pascual, Tony B. *Day Care Centers*. New York: Rand Corporation, 1969.

Policy Papers. The U.S. Department of Health, Education and Welfare. Unpublished. The U.S. Department of Health, Education and Welfare and Office of

Economic Opportunity and Agency for Children, Youth and Families, formerly Office of Child Development. These papers include over 100 memos, papers, and plans for child care policies.

Schultze, Charles L.; Fried, Edward R.; Rivlin, Alice M.; and Teeters, Nancy H. *Setting National Priorities: The 1973 Budget.* Washington, D.C.: The Brookings Institution, 1972.

Steiner, Gilbert Y., with the assistance of Milius, Pauline H. *The Children's Cause.* Washington, D.C.: The Brookings Institution, 1976.

Swenson, Janet P. *Alternatives in Quality Care: A Guide for Thinking and Planning.* Washington, D.C.: The Day Care and Child Development Council of America, 1972.

U.S. Department of Health, Education and Welfare. Head Start. *Statistical Highlights from the National Child Care Study* (DHEW Publication No. OHDO 76–31096). Washington, D.C.: Department of Health, Education and Welfare, 1976.

U.S. Office of Economic Opportunity. *Federal Interagency Day Care Requirements.* Department of Health, Education and Welfare. Washington, D.C.: Office of Economic Opportunity. Department of Labor, September 23, 1968.

U.S. Office of Economic Opportunity. Office of Program Development. *An Impact Study of Day Care: Feasibility Report and Manual for Community Planners.* Cambridge, Mass.: Center for the Study of Public Policy, 1971.

Westinghouse Learning Corporation and Westat Research. *Day Care Survey — 1970 Summary Report and Basic Analysis.* Prepared for Evaluation Divisions, Office of Economic Opportunity, Washington, D.C., April 1971.

Chapter Six: One Community's Trials and Travails

Aikman, William F. *Day Care Legal Handbook: Legal Aspects of Organizing & Operating Day Care Programs.* Urbana, Ill.: ERIC Clearinghouse on Early Childhood Education, University of Illinois, September 1977.

Bergstrom, Joan M., and Morgan, Gwen. *Issues in the Design of a Delivery System for Day Care and Child Development Services to Children and Their Families.* Boston: Wheelock College, May 1975.

Center for the Study of Parent Involvement. *State Education Agencies and Parent Involvement: A National Survey of State Legislation and the Policies and Perspectives of State Departments of Education.* Berkeley, Calif.: Center for the Study of Parent Involvement, February 1974.

Child Welfare League of America. *Day Care — An Expanding Resource for Children.* New York: Child Welfare League of America, 1967.

Day Care and Child Development Council of America. *Getting it Together.* Washington, D.C.: Office of Child Development, Department of Health, Education and Welfare, 1971.

Emlen, Arthur C. "Realistic Planning for the Day Care Consumer" and "Social Work Practice." *Selected Papers of National Conference on Social Welfare*, 97th annual forum. New York: Columbia University Press, June 5, 1970, p. 127.

Morgan, Gwen. *An Evaluation of the 4C Concept*. Washington, D.C.: Day Care and Child Development Council of America, February 1972.

National Institute of Mental Health. Department of Health, Education and Welfare. "Programs in Child Development and Child Care." *National Conference on Child Care*. Pittsburgh, Pa.: University of Pittsburgh, Western Psychiatric Institute and Clinic, May 20-23, 1969.

Zamoff, Richard B. *Guide to the Assessment of Day Care Services and Needs at the Community Level*. Washington, D.C.: The Urban Institute, July 1971.

Chapter Seven: Child Care Alternatives

Advisory Commission on the Status of Women. *Transcript of the Public Hearing on Day Care*, held jointly with Senate and Assembly Social Welfare Committees of the California Legislature. Public Health Building, San Francisco, October 17-18, 1968.

Assembly Office of Research. *California Children: Who Cares?* Sacramento, Calif.: Assembly Office of Research, 1974.

Bay Area Social Planning Council. "Child Day Care Services in the San Francisco Bay Area." Report prepared for United Bay Area Crusade. Oakland, Calif., September 20, 1974

Board of Supervisors, Child Care Initiative Task Force. "Implementation Plan for Child Care Services in San Francisco." San Francisco: Board of Supervisors, June 21, 1976.

Bourne, Patricia G., et al. *Day Care Nightmare*. Berkeley: Institute of Urban and Regional Development, University of California, February 1971.

California Child Day Care Licensing Task Force. The Office of Educational Liaison, State of California. *Report and Recommendations*. Sacramento, Calif., May 31, 1975.

California Commission on the Status of Women. *Child Care Issues for California*. California Commission on the Status of Women, March 1975.

Castro, Susan W. "The Impediments to Public Day Care Programs in San Francisco," an unpublished study, 1975.

Class, Norris E. *Growing Up in the 70's*. Sacramento, Calif.: California Legislature, August 1975.

Early Childhood Project. Education Commission of the States. *The Role of the Family in Child Development: Implications for State Policies and Programs*. Report No. 15. Denver, Colo: Education Commission of the States, 1975.

Early Childhood Project. Education Commission of the States. *State Services in*

Child Development: Needs Assessment and Planning, Child Abuse, Day Care Issues. Denver, Colo: Education Commission of the States, 1975.

Early Childhood Task Force. Education Commission of the States. *Early Childhood Development: Alternatives for Program Implementation in the States.* Denver, Colo.: Education Commission of the States, 1973.

Office of Educational Liaison, The; State of California. *Child Care: The Final Report.* Sacramento, Calif.: The Office of Educational Liaison, December 1975.

"Parents Fight to Keep Day Care Center Open." *San Francisco Examiner,* September 1, 1978, p. 4.

Post, A. Alan. Legislative Analyst. *Publicly Subsidized Child Care Services in California.* Sacramento, Calif.: State of California, August 23, 1974.

Urban Management Consultants of San Francisco. *Draft Report Children's Services: A Review of Intergovernmental Service Deliver Issues in California.* San Francisco, Calif.: Urban Management Consultants, March 11, 1975.

Chapter 8: What's Next?

Fairfield, Roy P. *Humanizing the Workplace.* Buffalo, N.Y.: Prometheus Books, 1974.

Featherstone, Joseph. "Kentucky Fried Chicken." *The New Republic,* September 5, 1970.

Gottschalk, Earl C., Jr. "Women at Work, Day Care is Booming, But Experts Are Split Over Its Effect on Kids." *The Wall Street Journal,* September 15, 1978.

Inner City Fund. *Potential Cost and Economic Benefits of Industrial Day Care.* Washington, D.C.: U.S. Department of Labor, May 1971.

"The Preschool Industry." *Bulletin.* Boston: Arthur D. Little, April 1970.

"Romper Room Schools: An Association of Creative Nursery Schools and Day-Care Centers." A Division of Romper Room Enterprises. A Subsidiary of Hasbro Industries, Rumford, R.I.

INDEX

INDEX